If God is so good why are things so bad?

The problem of suffering from Job to Jesus

Melvin Tinker

EP BOOKS (Evangelical Press)
Registered Office: 140 Coniscliffe Road,
Darlington, Co Durham, UK DL3 7RT

www.epbooks.org
admin@epbooks.org

EP Books are distributed in the USA by:
JPL Books, 3883 Linden Ave. S.E.,
Wyoming, MI 49548

www.jplbooks.com
orders@jplbooks.com

First EP Books edition published 2019.

ISBN: 978-1-78397-235-7

British Library Cataloguing in Publication Data available

Here is a book for the valley of the 'absence' of God, a book that can make us more compassionate in our counselling, more informed in our suffering, more faithful in our grieving, more comforted in our anguish, and more knee-prone in our worship; and it's a book with an 'after-life'—it raises matters that we, like Mary, will go on treasuring up in our hearts. And yet Melvin Tinker has cloaked these hard and heavy matters in such a clear and readable style.

Dr Dale Ralph Davies, Former Professor of Old Testament,
Reformed Theological Seminary, Jackson, Mississippi

Melvin Tinker writes with a theologian's mind, a Biblical scholar's attention to detail and a pastor's heart to minister. Using real life stories, he puts the book of Job under life's microscope to find practical insights that help us in times of suffering.

Mark Lanier, Author of *Christianity on Trial*

In an age when the petulant celebrity manchild with a passing acquaintance of suffering passes for a philosopher, Melvin Tinker opens the Book of Job in all its realism. Genuine comfort and true righteousness emerge. Compassionately and honestly caring for the suffering, he lets God be God—in Jesus.

Dr Steffen Jenkins, Tutor in Biblical Studies,
UNION School of Theology

Whilst there are no easy answers to suffering, this book provides an invaluable framework through which to engage with the problem of pain. *If God is so good why are things so bad* is a rare combination of careful exegesis, doctrinal clarity and Christ-centred theology. Melvin Tinker writes as someone who has clearly wrestled with the question of suffering and applies his material both as a pastorally sensitive preacher and an evangelistically compelling apologist. Christians, churches, and non-believers alike will benefit immensely from this book.

Revd Tony Jones, Christ Church, Durham

For Scott Mckay,
dear friend and colleague, with gratitude for
a decade of Gospel ministry together.

Contents

Foreword

Our world is a strange mix. We see so much beauty and goodness. Bird song lifts our spirits. Fictional stories move us to tears. An act of kindness can take us by surprise.

But our world is also scarred by anguish and evil. The death of a loved one leaves a hole that cannot readily be filled. Illness brings not only pain, but also frustration. Fractured relationships cause emotional turmoil. And when we look further afield we find these individual traumas scaled up beyond imagination as whole nations are torn apart by war, famine and disease.

For anyone engaging with the Christian message, suffering is a big question: How can an all-powerful, all-loving God allow suffering? Suffering appears to point to a God who is either indifferent to our plight or impotent to remedy it.

But suffering is also personal. For many of us it is not

some abstract conundrum, but a daily challenge. And to the challenge of coping is added the challenge of faith. Does God care for me?

In the book of Job these questions are not side-stepped. Job is the epitome of an innocent sufferer, crying out in confusion, demanding answers from God, expressing his confusion with raw, uncensored emotion. His friends pitch in with their theories, and the conversation rages backwards and forwards until finally God himself speaks. The book addresses the issue of suffering face on with a message that takes us by surprise.

Melvin Tinker invites us to walk with Job through the confusion sufferings creates. *If God is so good why are things so Bad* is like a guidebook, helping us navigate through unfamiliar territory.

It is a book for all those who suffer. Don't worry, you will not be offered glib platitudes or quick fixes. Here is a context in which you can express your pain honestly. But here, too, is a context in which your questions are brought to God rather them leading you away from God. What we are offered in this book is not so much a theory or a solution, but God himself.

But it is also a book for those who do *not* suffer. Here its message is just as important. For in the book of Job we see the danger of half-truths wielded without empathy. Job's supposed comforters often speak the truth. But they rarely speak the whole truth.

The result brings misery to Job and ultimately the censure from God (along with mercy). Yet this is a failing to which we are so easily prone. In our pride we confidently we think we know what's what. But, like a carpenter using a hammer on a screw, our half-truths do more harm than good. What we can do is give people Christ and this is what this book will help you do.

If God is so good why are things so Bad will help you understand the message of Job. But even more importantly it will help you put its message to good use—in your own life and in the life of others.

Tim Chester
Pastor of Grace Church, Boroughbridge, North Yorkshire
Faculty member of Crosslands Training

Preface

HE WAS DESPERATELY THIRSTY. THE SIGHT OF A FAT icicle hanging outside his hut in Auschwitz concentration camp caused Prisoner 174517 to reach out his hand in the hope of assuaging his thirst. Just before he could place it in his mouth, one of the guards snatched it out of his hand and ground it into the dirt.

'Warum?'—'Why?' the prisoner cried in astonished disbelief.

'Heir ist kein warum' replied the guard, 'Here there is no why.'

The prisoner in question was Primo Levi who later wrote, 'If there is an Auschwitz then there can be no God.' Does experiencing such monumental evil and suffering necessarily entail atheism?[1]

Someone else who was in Auschwitz was Victor Frankl who came to an altogether different conclusion: 'The truth is that amongst those who actually went through the experience of Auschwitz, the number of those whose religious life was deepened—in spite, not to say because of this experience—by far exceeds those who gave up their belief.'[2]

Frankl made the observation that as a weak flame can easily be blown out by a small breeze, so a weak faith might be extinguished quickly when it encounters suffering and evil; by the same token, real faith, like a strong flame, can be fanned into an inextinguishable flame by a storm.

Long before Levi and Frankl, there was Job who in his sufferings faced the extreme test of faith. Socrates is famously said to have remarked, 'The unexamined life is not worth living.' This was given an extra twist by the Stoic philosopher, Epictetus who wrote that, 'A life not put to the test is not worth living.' In Job we see a life sorely tested and deeply examined. Levi's tortured cry, 'Why?' appears more than once in this book. Some, like Job's friends attempt a simplistic, and often times, brutal explanation which is grotesquely reductionistic: good things happen to good people and bad things to bad people—an explanation sorely put to the test in the drama of debate which steadily unfolds.

The suffering undergone by Job appears from his standpoint to be pointless and inexplicable. Perhaps this is why Job is held out by many to be our 'suffering brother,' for his experience resonates with Auschwitz survivors like Levi, Frankl and, as we shall see, Wiesel, as well as those who have undergone suffering which is less extreme but no less real.

While there is much to learn from the Book of Job of what 'faith seeking understanding' is meant to look like in the midst of disorientating suffering, as well as the nature and purpose of pain in a fallen world, it would be a serious misreading of the book to fail to see that it is primarily a book from God about God. The Jewish literary critic George Steiner once remarked that on a good day at work he could go home and imagine Shakespeare sitting down and writing his plays. But, said Steiner, he could not imagine the same about the speeches of God in Job.[3] Here is something which goes beyond human insight. True wisdom allows God to be God in his apparent silence as well as his speeches, working behind the scenes as well as within them, using secondary agents to bring about his sovereign purposes as well as being personally present in the whirlwind. Of course, within the grand sweep of Scripture there comes a point in history where God himself becomes our 'suffering brother' in the person of Jesus Christ whom Job prefigures.

What follows is a series of expositions which attempt to walk the way of wisdom with Job so that we might learn to think and speak of God aright when hard times come our way. I wholeheartedly agree with Eric Ortlund when he writes, 'I believe the book of Job speaks directly to faithful sufferers in ways that, if not simple, are clear and encouraging.' He goes on to say, 'The book of Job is a greatly underused resource for endurance in discipleship in the midst of deep pain.'[4] It is hoped this book will go some small way towards correcting that.

Melvin Tinker,
St John Newland,
2018
Soli Deo Gloria

1 *When Bad Things Happen to Good People*

Job 1–2

It was just over 70 years ago that Auschwitz concentration camp was liberated by the Soviet Army in 1945. One of those discovered half starved to death was a fifteen year old Hungarian Jew named Elie Wiesel. He, his mother and sister were separated at the camp, and would not see each other again. He wrote: 'Never shall I forget that night, the first night of the camp, which has turned my life into one long night, seven times cursed and seven times sealed. Never shall I forget that smoke, never shall I forget those flames which consumed my faith forever ... Never shall I forget those moments which murdered my God and my soul and turned my dreams to dust. Some talked of God, of his mysterious ways, of the sins of the Jewish people, and of their future deliverance. But I ceased to pray. How I sympathised with Job! I did not deny God's existence, but I doubted his absolute justice.'[1]

Given what he saw in Auschwitz such a doubt is perfectly understandable, and some would say, wholly justifiable:

> The other gas chambers were full of the adults and therefore the children were not gassed, but just burned alive. There were several thousand of them. When one of the SS sort of had pity upon the children, he would take the child and beat the head against a stone before putting it on the pile of fire and wood, so the child lost consciousness. However, the regular way they did it was by just throwing the children onto the pile. They would put a sheet of wood there, then sprinkle the whole thing with petrol, then wood again, and petrol and wood, and petrol—then they placed the children there. Then the whole thing would be ignited.'[2]

The cry behind the cry

Behind the cry 'Where is God?' is the deeper cry of Wiesel, 'Where is God's justice? Why doesn't he do something? Surely if he is all powerful he can, and if he is all good he will, so why the delay?' Some would argue that this is the price we have to pay for having what is called 'free will.' We can choose to do good or evil and innocents invariably get caught up as collateral damage when evil is chosen. Others would maintain that if that is so then the price for such 'free will' is way too high—for example, six million Jews disappearing in the gas chambers and sixty million lives perishing in World War Two.[3]

But what of situations which don't involve the action of other human beings but 'creation gone wrong,' as was the case with another Jewish believer, Rabbi Harold Kushner? His son, Aaron, had been diagnosed with a rapid ageing disease, becoming like an old man of eighty. Kushner writes: 'I believed that I was following God's ways and doing his work. How could this be happening to my family? If God existed, if he was minimally fair, let alone loving and forgiving, how could he do this to me? And even if I could persuade myself that I deserved this punishment for some sin of neglect or pride that I was not aware of, what grounds did Aaron have to suffer?'[4]

Perhaps even more candid in his questioning is Philip Yancey, 'If God is truly in charge, somehow connected to all the world's suffering, why is he so capricious, unfair? Is he the cosmic sadist who delights in watching us squirm?'[5]

Senseless suffering

Perhaps of all the books in the Bible associated with the question of senseless suffering, what philosophers call 'the surd,' the book of Job is the most well-known and yet least understood. It is a book which doesn't deal primarily with the 'why' question of the origins of evil and suffering (although we are given some insights into these as we shall see) but deals more with the practical 'how' questions, that is, how are we to think of God when we suffer? How can we face up to the fact that we live in a broken, fallen world which means that no matter how good we are, things are going to cross our path which will hurt us and those we love? In such situations not only do we need to think about God rightly but *speak* of him properly.[6]

The book of Job is part of what is called 'wisdom literature,' and wisdom is primarily about how to live life and negotiate its challenges wisely, including the challenge of enduring intolerable pain.[7] This is one of the main purposes of the book of Job, to help us know why we can trust God who knows why even when we don't.[8] Unlike, for example, the Book of Ecclesiastes, Job is not dealing with the problem of pain as something which is primarily an intellectual problem, but as something experiential. How do *I* cope with such suffering together with my faith in God?

It is no accident that the book focuses on an individual because that is how we have to deal with suffering—as an *individual* experience. It is also deliberate that after the prologue setting the scene in chapters 1 and 2, which is written in Hebrew prose equivalent to that written by a thirteen year old, it is followed by forty or so chapters of the most sublime poetic writing, equivalent to Shakespeare and then reverts back again in the last chapter.[9] This may be because while we often experience suffering at the level of everyday mundane affairs, when we try and ponder losing our wealth, our health and our family, we find ourselves in deep, unchartered and turbulent waters—like moving from reading a story written by a thirteen year old to reading Shakespeare. What is more, reading the forty odd chapters of Job and his critics going back and forth in accusation and defence can seem interminable; does it not feel like that when you are in the midst of anguished suffering, it just seems to go on and on with no end in sight? It is also significant that with the possible exception of one character, none of the others, including Job, are Jewish, pointing to the fact that in different ways and with varying depths this is the experience of every person: believers are not exempt.

When all is well

We are introduced to the main protagonist, Job, in chapter 1, 'There was a man in the land of Uz whose name was Job, and that man was blameless and upright, one who feared God and turned away from evil. There were born to him seven sons and three daughters. He possessed 7,000 sheep, 3,000 camels, 500 yoke of oxen, and 500 female donkeys, and very many servants, so that this man was the greatest of all the people of the east.'

The name 'Job' means 'ill-treated one' (from *ayabh*) or 'converted one' (from *yubh*). He is presented as living at a time when a person's wealth was measured not in terms of the size of their bank balance but the size of their herds. This would place him in the period of the Hebrew patriarchs, with men like Abraham, Isaac and Jacob. What is more, we are told he lived in Uz, which would locate the story somewhere between what today would be southern Jordan and south-central Iraq. He is therefore well beyond the bounds of Israel, but nonetheless he fears the God of Israel—Yahweh, and the fear of God, as we are told in Proverbs, is 'the beginning of wisdom' (Proverbs 9:10).

Job's religious and moral credentials are established as impeccable from the very beginning. He was 'blameless and upright, one who feared God and turned away from evil.' Not only is Job great morally but materially with the numbers of children and belongings thus reflecting Old Testament symbolism of completeness (threes, sevens and tens). We are told he was the greatest man in the East by whichever measure you may care to use.

His deep personal piety showed itself in several ways, not least in his passionate concern for the spiritual well-being of his children. In verses 4–5 we read that just in case his sons and daughters had behaved in a way which might have offended God and brought down his judgement upon them, Job went out of his way to make sacrifices for their sin on their behalf:

> His sons used to go and hold a feast in the house of each one on his day, and they would send and invite their three sisters to eat and drink with them. And when the days of the feast had run their course, Job would send and consecrate them, and he would

rise early in the morning and offer burnt offerings according to the number of them all. For Job said, 'It may be that my children have sinned, and cursed God in their hearts.'

Neither was this a passing fad for Job for we are told that Job did this continually—Job was persistent in his parenting.

However, maybe here we begin to see some small flaw in his character, a weakness which needs to be challenged and strengthened which might only come through suffering. Later in chapter 3:25, after everything has been taken away from Job, we hear him saying: 'For the thing that I fear comes upon me, and what I dread befalls me.' Perhaps this in part explains why he seemed so obsessive in offering sacrifices for his children. Deep down Job was plagued with fear and uncertainty about the future.[10] And so in spite of his well-ordered and secure existence, life was a little more unpredictable and uncertain than he perhaps dare openly admit. In which case why not trust God for the future rather than trying to control the future?

This is a challenge we all face, especially those of us who occupy the more anxious side of the anxiety-contentment spectrum with regard to our families. Making proper arrangements for them is one thing, going over the top and worrying about them is another. As our world seems to become more unpredictable being able to trust in the God who holds the future in his hands will become increasingly important for us.

Without doubt on a relative scale of values Job does appear to stand head and shoulders above everyone else as affirmed by God himself in verse 8, underscoring verse 1 that he is blameless in character and upright in action. Here is a sincere worshipper of Yahweh, an honest hard-working businessman, a loving husband and thoughtful father who is second to none. For some Job almost appears to be too good to be true. But as we shall see, Job is one of those rare individuals which exist within a class all by themselves, *sui generis*; he is a genuinely good man.

The drama of death

What could possibly go wrong? The scene switches from the everyday affairs of earth to the unseen Divine court in heaven where an angelic being called the 'Satan' arrives in God's presence. The word 'Satan' is not a proper name like 'Bill,' rather it is a description of the creature's role; it means 'accuser'[11] or 'prosecutor,' we might even say, 'challenger.'[12] What we are to note is that the angelic barrister does not accuse Job of doing anything wrong, except maybe having dubious motives for living a godly life; rather it is God who is being harangued for setting up a phony arrangement amongst human beings by blessing righteous behaviour with rewards, and this, the Satan argues, hampers true righteousness. This underlies what some have called the 'retribution principle,' the 'conviction that the righteous will prosper and the wicked will suffer, both in proportion to their respective righteousness and wickedness.'[13] The assumption is that real righteousness involves doing good and honouring God for their own sake, not because of what we might get out of them. This is the first charge levelled against God: 'Does Job fear God for no reason? Have you not put a hedge around him and his house and all that he has, on every side? You have blessed the work of his hands ... But stretch out your hand and touch all that he has, and he will curse you to your face.' (v.9–11). 'The only reason why Job behaves as he does,' argues the Challenger, 'is because he knows on which side his bread is buttered. He is religious and moral only because of what he can get out of it. After all, everyone knows that religion is nothing but enlightened self-interest. It's just a matter of the right carrot and stick with Job. In fact, you can put it all down to his rather fortunate circumstances which you, God, have provided. Anybody can afford to be religious when they have a lifestyle like that!' The underlying point is that with this kind of arrangement one can never truly know whether people are being genuinely righteous for righteousness's sake or simply being good in order to enjoy blessings. In short, the Satan is charging God with setting up a defective system. There is only one way to find out, he argues, and that is to put Job to the test by taking away some of his benefits.

Accordingly, God allows the Satan to do his worst. Perhaps not quite his worst, because in the first instance God will not permit Job to be physically harmed. The Satan can go so far but no further; God still remains sovereign in setting limits. 'And the LORD said to Satan, "Behold, all that he has is in your hand. Only against him do not stretch out your hand"' (v.12).

A world falling apart

In what has all the components of a screaming nightmare, Job's life is totally wasted.

The first thing to disintegrate is Job's financial empire: raiders attack his oxen, donkeys and camels, carrying them off and killing his servants. This is followed by the fire of God which falls from the sky and burns up the sheep and the servants (vv.14–17). This is an economic disaster of epic proportions. But even that catastrophe is nothing compared to the devastating news which comes hard on its heels: Job's children were all in the same house when a storm hit with deadly force, 'Your sons and daughters were eating and drinking wine in their oldest brother's house, and behold, a great wind came across the wilderness and struck the four corners of the house, and it fell upon the young people, and they are dead, and I alone have escaped to tell you!' (vv.18–19).

How might we have responded? Here is Job's response: 'Then Job arose and tore his robe and shaved his head [signs of intense grief and mourning] and fell on the ground and worshiped. And he said, "Naked I came from my mother's womb, and naked shall I return. The LORD gave, and the LORD has taken away; blessed be the name of the LORD"' (vv.20–22).

We may think that that would be enough for any man to bear. God apparently thinks not. As the veil is lifted once more on the invisible world in chapter 2, we find ourselves in the heavenly court yet again, only to discover the wager being taken one stage further. The Challenger, still not convinced that there is not a base ulterior motive for Job's faith, pursues his case in verses 4–5: 'Skin for skin! All that a man has he will give for his life. But stretch out your hand and touch his bone and his flesh, and he will curse you to your face.' In other words, 'Get under Job's skin, God, and let him feel some physical suffering; let him think that his own life is being threatened and then watch him reveal his true colours and you will discover that he is only out for himself.'

Job is afflicted with boils causing such excruciating pain that his wife, finding it unbearable to watch, urges Job to commit voluntary euthanasia by cursing God, 'Then his wife said to him, "Do you still hold fast your integrity? Curse God and die"' (v.9). It might well be that the wife's advice is a faint echo of Eve's counsel to Adam in the Garden of Eden (and here we have another man like Adam who initially, at least, appears to be in his own garden paradise, one which is fast unravelling). In both stories the woman's advice follows the Challenger and leads towards death.[14] However, Job's response is unlike that of Adam, '"You speak as one of the foolish women would speak. Shall we receive good from God, and shall we not receive evil?" In all this Job did not sin with his lips' (v.10).

Job is so despairing and disfigured that when his friends, Eliphaz, Bildad and Zophar, arrive to console him they hardly recognise him as the same man and fell down into uncontrollable weeping, 'And when they saw him from a distance, they did not recognize him. And they raised their voices and wept, and they tore their robes and sprinkled dust on their heads toward heaven. And they sat with him on the ground seven days and seven nights, and no one spoke a word to him, for they saw that his suffering was very great' (vv.12–13).

The fight of faith

Here was a man undergoing suffering alright, suffering which was heightened, not lessened, by his faith in God. For if he had not believed in God it would have been some cold comfort to know that it was all a result of blind Chance with no-one to blame. But for Job to believe in God, and a good and all powerful God at that, seems to fly in the face of his present experience. How could such a God allow this to happen? If God has set up his world in terms of cause and effect in the physical realm, with a parallel system of cause and effect in the spiritual and moral realm—good things happen to good people and bad things happen to bad people— how is one to go about explaining what is happening to Job who is one of the good people? As we shall see, this is Job's troubling question with which he wrestles throughout the remainder of the book. Of course it raises a prior question as to whether God *does* operate a kind of 'tit for tat' system which some Christians today think he does or at least should.

The great man is reduced by great suffering to a simpering, pitiful, but still believing, wreck as he crawls onto the ash heap to die wishing he had never been born, 'Why did I not die at birth, come out from the womb and expire? Why did the knees receive me? Or why the breasts, that I should nurse?' (3:11).

One of the main lessons in confronting the problem of pain is to realise there is an irreducible element of mystery in all suffering. Job's cry was 'Why?' 'Why didn't I die at birth?' 'Why was I not stillborn?' 'Why is light given to those in misery?' Job is never given the answers. Although we as readers are allowed to have some insight into what is going on in the heavenly realm, providing a wider context of meaning, Job is not. He is never made aware of the discussion between God and the Satan. This is important, for one of the main themes of this book is the need to trust God in situations when we do not know why certain things are happening. Nonetheless let it be said that this faith of Job is not blind faith. Job knew about God, he had reasons to believe that God is all powerful and all good, and is reminded of these things later when he encounters God as described in chapters 38–42. Therefore, although Job did not know why these things were happening to him, he did know enough about God to know why he trusted him who did know why. But as suffering progresses, how is one to think of God then? This too is something Job will struggle with intensely.

Knowing enough about God who does know all the answers while we don't is crucial in enabling us to endure what St John of the Cross called the 'dark night of the soul.'

This is movingly illustrated by a story told by Professor D.A. Carson.[15] It concerns a young man who was a six foot skinny something who worked in Latin America for about fifteen years as an effective church planter and ministry trainer. He met his wife, who was a daughter of a missionary family, while overseas. In due course they were blessed with the birth of a baby girl. The missionary agency to which the church planter belonged wanted him to gain a doctorate so that he could be more effective in training. Subsequently he embarked on a course at Trinity Evangelical Divinity School where D.A. Carson served as a professor. Six months into the course his wife was diagnosed with stage 4 breast cancer. She underwent the usual treatment: a mastectomy and chemotherapy—fighting for her life. Wonderfully, she came through it all and for a while it looked as if she had been cured. The husband started up his studies again. Six months later he was diagnosed with advanced stomach cancer. The local hospitals, which were good ones, said there was nothing they could do for him. The mission board eventually sent him to the Mayo clinic which suggested a course of treatment which involved taking out ninety percent of his stomach and supplying him with drugs which were normally used for colon cancer. Six months later, skinnier than ever, eating around ten times a day, he resumed his studies. Six months afterwards his wife's cancer returned. Soon, she was dead.

Eventually he came back to Trinity Evangelical Divinity School to complete his PhD. The last time Dr Carson saw him, his daughter was nine and a half, and they were getting ready to go back to Latin America. He came to address the church Dr Carson attends. As he spoke that Sunday morning for about half an hour, all he talked about was the goodness of God. How could he do that? The short answer is that he really did know the God who knew why.

2 *Correctness over Compassion*

Job 3–41

THE FRENCH ATHEIST, JEAN PAUL SARTRE WROTE A play entitled *The Devil and the Good Lord* in which the main character was a butchering soldier, Goetz, who decided to give up his murderous ways and become a Christian. As the play proceeds, Goetz becomes increasingly disillusioned with what he considers to be God's silence. He finally bursts out: 'I prayed, I demanded a sign. I sent messages to heaven, no reply. Heaven ignored my very name. Each minute I wondered what I could be in the eyes of God. Now I know the answer: nothing. God does not see me. God does not hear me. God does not know me. You see this emptiness over our heads? That is God. You see this gap in the door? It is God. You see that hole in the ground?

That is God again. Silence is God. Absence is God. God is the loneliness of man.'

Joseph Parker was the minister of the City Temple in London, from 1874 until his death in 1902. He said that up to the age of sixty-eight he had never had a religious doubt, but then his wife died and his faith all but collapsed. He wrote: 'In that dark hour, I became almost an atheist. For God had set his foot upon my prayers and treated my petitions with contempt. If I had seen a dog in such agony as mine, I would have pitied and helped the dumb beast; yet God spat upon me and cast me out as an offence—out into the waste wilderness and the night black and starless.'[1]

Where is God when your world is falling apart? Why doesn't he say something? Why doesn't he do something, even if it is simply putting an end to the misery by taking away our life? Those are the cries of men like Sartre and Parker, and they may have been your cries too. They were certainly the heartfelt pleas of Job.

Job the model of godliness, the paradigm of virtue, kindness itself, is now reduced to a pathetic, tormented figure shivering on the local dung hill. His livelihood is in ruins, his family devastated and his health all but broken. In fact, he has very little left save two things: his faith—just, and his integrity (2:9). In the central sections of the book both of these come under a blistering attack from, would you believe, three of his closest friends. As we consider their counsel we may well think that with friends like these who needs enemies!

Sincere but sincerely wrong

It has to be said, however, that no matter how crass, misleading and insensitive Job's three counsellors— Eliphaz, Bildad and Zophar—prove to be, their intentions were nonetheless sincere. In their own way they represent a certain type of Christian who is to be found today. If we wanted to summarise their position it would be: 'My mind is made up—don't confuse me with the facts. I have my theology and I am sticking to it.' Even before Job opens his mouth they have already decided what the real problem is and where the problem lies. The problem is sin and it lies with Job. It can't be God's fault for he wouldn't do such a thing without a reason, and the only reason they could see for God inflicting such suffering is in judgement. Judgement upon what? Upon Job's sin, of course!

On the other hand, there is Job who also represents a certain group of Christians. If we were to characterise his position it could be in the words of a John Lennon song: 'Gimme some truth.' Job is in effect saying to his friends: 'I don't want your tight theology, however logical it may seem to you. I want to get to the bottom of what is really going on. I want the truth. More than that, I want to meet the God of Truth so that he can vindicate me before the world. To suffer physical pain and family loss is one thing, but to suffer false accusations of being a liar, a cheat and deserving what is happening, as my friends are saying, is one pain too many and only God can put it right.' That is the burden of these chapters.

The case in court

What we are introduced to in these central sections is a 'philosophical courtroom.' The way things develop is in the way judicial business would have been conducted in an ancient Near Eastern trial. We are to remember that everyone is buying into the retribution theory: good is rewarded and evil is punished and that is how God shows he is just—so they think. Three claims are being laid out: 1. God is just, 2. Job is righteous, and 3. The retribution principle is true. However, all three can't be right at the same time in this instance. At least one of them has to be jettisoned for the tension to be relieved. The question is: which one? Or putting it another way: who or what is to be proved false—God, Job or the retribution principle?

The way the next stage in the drama is set out is as follows: each of Job's friends in turn attacks him verbally. After each assault Job defends himself. This cycle of attack, defence and counter-attack is repeated three times, until eventually Job explodes in one long outburst, reducing his friends to silence. Even then he still does not succeed in convincing them that he is innocent. Their minds were made up and they didn't want to be confused by the facts.

Their reasoning was quite simple and went something like this: all suffering is due to wickedness. Job is suffering, therefore he is wicked—QED. What could be simpler? We see this in Eliphaz's speech in 4:7–9: 'Remember: who that was innocent ever perished? Or where were the upright cut off? As I have seen, those who plow iniquity and sow trouble reap the same. By the breath of God they perish …'

The retribution principle

Eliphaz prides himself in being an astute observer of human affairs; 'Everyone knows, Job, that God has ordered the world in terms of moral cause and effect. If you are good you prosper, if you are bad, then eventually your sins will find you out. You can't escape it, any more than you can escape the law of gravity; it's immutable. You reap what you sow.' The implication is left hanging in the air that Job must have sown some rather destructive seeds to be suffering this much.

Furthermore, Eliphaz claims that he has had a special revelation confirming this viewpoint—a vision, and who can argue with that?:

Now a word was brought to me stealthily; my ear received the whisper of it. Amid thoughts from visions of the night, when deep sleep falls on men, dread came upon me, and trembling, which made all my bones shake. A spirit glided past my face; the hair of my flesh stood up. It stood still, but I could not discern its appearance. A form was before my eyes; there was silence, then I heard a voice: 'Can mortal man be in the right before God? Can a man be pure before his Maker?' (4:12–17)

The very way Job's friend's speeches are couched appear rather thin in terms of their poetry let alone theology compared to that of Job who towers above them like a colossus and whose speeches are only outshone by God's in the last few chapters.

Here is part of Job's response in chapter 9:5ff (compare his vision of the grandeur of God with that of his friends or even ours), 'he who removes mountains, and they know it not, when he overturns them in his anger, who shakes the earth out of its place, and its pillars tremble; who commands the sun, and it does not rise; who seals up the stars; who alone stretched out the heavens and trampled the waves of the sea.' These men are spiritual pygmies compared to Job and yet they treat him as if he is the dumb one![2]

There is perhaps even more to the difference in the quality of the poetry than Job's spiritual superiority: 'The poetry illumines the stark disagreement of the two parties about the nature of God and his justice. The friends assume that God, being wholly good and all powerful, would never bring suffering to a righteous man. But we know that in this point they are totally deceived.' The words of Martin Luther to Erasmus might well apply to Job's friends, 'Your thoughts of God are all too human.'

The backing of tradition

The friends then bring out the big guns of religious tradition to blast Job as we see with Bildad in chapter 8:2–3, 8–10. 'How long will you say these things, and the words of your mouth be a great wind? Does God pervert justice? ... For inquire, please, of bygone ages, and consider what the fathers have searched out. For we are but of yesterday and know nothing, for our days on earth are a shadow. Will they not teach you and tell you and utter words out of their understanding?'

Putting it another way Bildad is arguing, 'This is no novel idea we are propounding as you well know Job. God operates according to strict justice. It is the received wisdom of our elders, men far wiser than you have come to this conclusion. So why don't you stop being so obstinate? Admit your sin and repent. Nothing could be simpler.'

Job, however, remains intransigent. No matter how 'sound' their ideas are, and Job admits they are in 9:1, 'Truly I know that it is so'—the theory does not do justice to the facts.[3] While it may be a rule of thumb that what a man sows, so shall he reap—live the life of a hell raiser and don't be surprised if you die of an overdose—that at least makes some sense. But that is not Job's situation and it is wrong to pretend otherwise.

The inquisition

Eventually, after listening to Job's special pleading,

which in itself may have confirmed his guilt in his friends' eyes (he protests too much), the third of his friends, Zophar, can't stomach any more. He knows what he believes and he is sticking with it and no matter how cutting and unkind his words may be, he is going to give Job a piece of his mind:

> Should a multitude of words go unanswered, and a man full of talk be judged right? Should your babble silence men, and when you mock, shall no one shame you? For you say, 'My doctrine is pure, and I am clean in God's eyes.' But oh, that God would speak and open his lips to you, and that he would tell you the secrets of wisdom! For he is manifold in understanding. Know then that God exacts of you less than your guilt deserves. (11:2–6)

In a torrent of rage, Zophar and his two colleagues are bullying Job into signing a false confession. This is an inquisition at work. 'Look,' he is arguing, 'you may be able to fool some people with this 'butter wouldn't melt in my mouth' story. But you don't fool God. If he were here he would soon put you in your place. Why, so great is your sin and so long is the list of them that even God couldn't keep a complete record, that's why he's forgotten some of them!'

Later, in 22:4–11, Eliphaz is even more merciless in skewering Job:

> Is it for your fear of him that he reproves you and enters into judgment with you? Is not your

evil abundant? There is no end to your iniquities. For you have exacted pledges of your brothers for nothing and stripped the naked of their clothing ... Therefore snares are all around you, and sudden terror overwhelms you, or darkness, so that you cannot see, and a flood of water covers you.

What we are being presented with is part of the 'plausibility structures' of the day, those background assumptions, beliefs and ways of thinking which are taken as 'given' by any society. '*Everyone* knows how certain rich men get their wealth—double dealing on the side, fiddling the books, exploiting the poor. So that's how you must have come upon your wealth, Job, and God has found you out and is now giving you your just deserts.' The solution each of them gives to Job is the same: come clean, repent and turn to God and be restored to your former prosperity. We see this for example in 22:21: 'Agree with God, and be at peace; thereby good will come to you.'

Too convenient

It has to be admitted that their theology is all very neat and tidy, admitting of no loose ends. It explained things remarkably well, so well in fact they didn't have to bother thinking for themselves as it was all done for them by their theory of retribution (*Vergeltung*). So what if some of the facts didn't seem to fit? They could either be conveniently ignored or forced to fit. But it seems a little too convenient. To the question:

'If God is so good then why are things so bad?' Job's comforters would answer 'it must be because you are so bad.' Steven Nation puts his finger on the weakness of the retribution theory when he writes, 'The idea of retributive theology does not defend God's goodness and justice and righteousness. On the contrary, they pigeonhole God into being a God who interacts in a cause-and-effect manner instead of the unique, mysterious and faithful God which His and Job's speeches declare (ch.38–42). Retributive theology is one major aspect of God's revelation in the book of Job which He wants to reject.'[4]

It is important to recognise that the Bible does teach that some suffering is punishment for sin (e.g. Romans 1:24ff and the 'giving over' of people to the consequences of their sin), but not all suffering is to be viewed in this way. What Job's friends were doing was mistaking part of the truth for the whole truth and the result was appallingly cruel. They add more suffering to one who is already at breaking point by trying to get him to abandon one of the few things left which is precious to him—his integrity. By this verbal arm twisting they aim to get him to say that which he does not believe to be true. But in so doing they also blind themselves, foreclosing on any possibility that their understanding might be in need of correction.

How not to be a 'comforter'

Here is a warning for us all: however sincere, we must be careful not to become a Job's 'comforter.'

To begin with, it is obvious that they really didn't hear what Job was saying, let alone heed it. For sure they heard his objections, but they gave them no real consideration. That would have hurt. When you are going through a crisis, suffering deep emotional pain, the last thing you want is for your own integrity to be violated, for someone to treat you as if you are less than human without thoughts or feelings but simply as an object to be assailed with 'the right answers.' It seems clear that whatever concerns these friends had for Job, those concerns were overridden by a greater concern, namely, to keep their own watertight beliefs intact. It was far more important to them that they should not allow their ideas to be brought into question than for truth to be pursued however uncomfortable that might be. Christians are not immune to this rather unfortunate habit of burying their heads in the sand instead of rigorously thinking something through.

What is perhaps worse is the cruelty of adding to a person's pain guilt which doesn't really belong there. A modern day example of this is what is called 'healing prosperity' or 'name it and claim it' teaching. It goes something like this: 'if you have an illness, have faith and you will be healed. If you are not healed it is because you haven't enough faith, or because your wife doesn't have enough faith, or because you great-uncle was a Freemason!'

Is this an exaggeration? Here is an account written by the late Professor Verna Wright, of a healing crusade at Horsforth in Leeds several years ago which exemplifies well this position:

> One night a friend of mine who is deaf in one ear thought he would have a go at being healed. Hands were laid upon him and he was told that he was healed, but he said, 'I am not.' The healer said, 'Yes, you are.' 'No, I am not,' my friend insisted, only to be told, 'well, it must be that you have not got sufficient faith.' After a brief altercation the healer went on down the line of deaf people. When the healing activities had finished my friend turned to the lady next to him and said, 'What did he do for you, love?' and she replied with her hand cupped to her ear, 'What did you say?' This would be almost comical if it were not so tragic! Think of the effects such haranguing had on those people.

This is a theology with no loose ends and which does not acknowledge there is such a thing as *innocent* suffering, and as a consequence multiplying pain by causing mental anguish.

However, this is not simply a danger for those whom we may consider to have extreme theologies, but also for those who value genuine theology arising from the Bible. Did you notice that Job's three friends are placing a lot of faith in their theology about God rather than exercising faith in God? They were willing to argue with Job but not pray for Job. In fact only Job is recorded of having prayed in this whole sorry episode, praying for these men to be forgiven! In Job 42:7, where God rebukes the three friends, it could be translated, 'You have not spoken to me as my servant Job has.' Unlike his friends, Job is a pray-er and not just a debater.[5]

Here lies an important lesson for those who highly prize the Bible and doctrine: beliefs and propositions can be advanced with great zeal which are wrong, or at least partially deficient. This is an instance of the wrong truths being applied to the wrong person at the wrong time, or as Edouard Dhorme puts it, 'His friends seek to apply normal solutions to the exceptional case.'[6] Who has not done this, maybe in a desire to defend God or Scripture against 'error'? In so doing the danger is winning the argument at the expense of losing the person. We need to be careful what we say and how we say it, lest we become a 'Job's comforter' as theological correctness is pursued at the expense of genuine compassion.

Character counts

Job, however, will have none of it. Whatever the majority might say, however unimpeachable their orthodoxy or whatever alleged 'special revelations' they have received, Job knows the truth about himself and will not sacrifice his integrity on the altar of expediency.

Although, like an innocent man after prolonged interrogation by his captors, it must have been tempting to give up and take the easy way out saying, 'OK, I admit I'm guilty, just let me out of this hell,' Job at least has the courage to say, 'No.' Whatever is going on, it is *not* his fault and he will not be brutalised into false humility by taking the rap for something he did not do:

> As God lives, who has taken away my right, and the Almighty, who has made my soul bitter, as long as my breath is in me, and the spirit of God is in my nostrils, my lips will not speak falsehood, and my tongue will not utter deceit. Far be it from me to say that you are right; till I die I will not put away my integrity from me. (27:2–5)

In chapters 29–31 Job gives a most moving recital of all the godly things he did before his world fell apart. He had been honest, disciplined, had rescued the poor, helped the blind, comforted those who mourned, and made a promise not to look lustfully at a girl. He opened his home to countless strangers, never rejoiced over other people's misfortunes and refused to trust in his own wealth.

What Job wanted was not some theoretical problem-solving of the 'Why does God allow suffering?' variety, which sceptics are so adept at asking. He wanted to meet with God. He wanted to hear God's voice and hear God's reason for allowing this appalling act of human misery:

I loathe my life; I will give free utterance to my complaint; I will speak in the bitterness of my soul. I will say to God, Do not condemn me; let me know why you contend against me. Does it seem good to you to oppress, to despise the work of your hands? (10:1–3)

Job turns to God to plead with him to show himself just for once and explain this injustice, for that is what Job is convinced it is. In a fit of deep depression he longs for the days when he knew God's kindness:

Oh, that I were as in the months of old, as in the days when God watched over me, when his lamp shone upon my head, and by his light I walked through darkness, as I was in my prime, when the friendship of God was upon my tent, when the Almighty was yet with me, when my children were all around me, when my steps were washed with butter, and the rock poured out for me streams of oil! (29:1–6)

This is profoundly moving. He wants to be with *God*. The astonishing thing is that although Job sails very close to the wind in bordering on blasphemy, he never ceases to believe. Not once does he slip over into atheism; it is not an option open to him:

Though he slay me, *I will hope in him*; yet I will argue my ways to his face. This will be my salvation, that the godless shall not come before him. (13:15–16, emphasis added)

He is so convinced of his innocence that he is willing to die if that is the only way he can come before God to vindicate himself for he is sure God will clear his name. But it is *God's* vindication he wants, not that of his friends. And, as we shall see his heart's desire would eventually be granted, but not until many more tears had been shed.

Like Job we too are not to be content with anything less than a personal knowledge of God. Don't be satisfied with theories about him, or sophisticated ideas about the problem of evil which in the end domesticate God and make light of his ways, settle for nothing less than God himself, however many tears we might have to shed in the process.

Seeking God

Where is such a God to be found? A God who is merciful and who understands? The answer: he is found, of all places, on a cross. If we really want to know what God is like and to have that intimacy of fellowship with him, then that is where we begin to look, at the God-man Jesus, who also knew the dark night of the soul, rejection and misunderstanding, even by his closest friends, and who, having gone through it all, now rules this broken world of ours in unremitting glory. In the words of the writer to the Hebrews, 'But we see him who for a little while was made lower than the angels, namely Jesus, crowned with glory and honour because of the suffering of death, so that by the grace of God he might taste death for everyone' (2:9).

One man who discovered this to be so in his own experience was John Owen.

He was one of the most influential Christians of his age. He had an intellect which was second to none, such that he became vice-chancellor of Oxford University no less and was involved in producing several theological masterpieces. That was in the first part of his life. Onward and upward (like Job), so it seemed. But then a new regime under a new King the 'merry monarch,' Charles II was established. As a consequence he lost his post, was forced into social exile and hampered and harassed by the new government. If that were not enough, he lived long enough to bury all of his eleven children, ten of whom died in infancy, together with the love of his life, his wife Mary. How is someone to cope with what seems to be a steady disintegration of their world? We are given a glimpse as to the answer by what Owen wrote after the death of his first ten children, 'a due contemplation of the glory of Christ will restore and compose the mind ... [it] will lift the minds and hearts of believers above all the troubles of this life, and is the sovereign antidote that will expel all the poison that is in them; which otherwise might perplex and enslave their souls.' Elsewhere he writes, 'Do any of us find decays in grace prevailing in us; deadness, coldness, lukewarmness, a kind of spiritual stupidity and senselessness coming upon us? ... Let us assure ourselves there is no better way for our healing and deliverance, indeed, no other way but this alone, namely, the obtaining a fresh view of the glory of Christ by faith, and a steady abiding in it. Constant contemplation of Christ, his glory, putting forth its transforming power is the revival of all grace and its only relief.'

Nothing less than a true knowledge of the true God will be sufficient, as Job was to discover, knowledge found in Christ.

3 Cosmos or Chaos?

Job 9

YOU MAY BE FAMILIAR WITH C.S. LEWIS'S ALLEGORY,[1] *The Lion, the Witch and the Wardrobe*. As the Pevensie children enter the magical land of Narnia for the first time, they meet Mr and Mrs Beaver, who describe to them the mighty lion, Aslan, the Christ-like figure of the series.

This is how the conversation goes:

'Is he a man?' asked Lucy.

'Aslan a man!' said Mr Beaver sternly. 'Certainly not. I tell you he is King of the wood and the son of the great emperor-beyond-the-sea. Don't you know who is the King of the Beasts? Aslan is a lion—the Lion, the great lion.'

'Ooh!' said Susan, 'I'd thought he was a man. Is

he—quite safe? I shall feel rather nervous about meeting a lion.'

'That you will, dearie, and no mistake,' said Mrs Beaver; 'if there's anyone who can appear before Aslan without their knees knocking, they're either braver than most or else just silly.'

'Then he isn't safe?' said Lucy.

'Safe?' said Mr Beaver; 'don't you hear what Mrs Beaver tells you? Who said anything about safe? 'Course he isn't safe. But he's good. He's the King, I tell you.'

In many ways that telling phrase takes us right to the heart of Job chapter 9. The 'safe' God of the opening paragraphs of the book and the 'safe' God of some of Job's counsellors who is so tame and predictable, no bigger than their puny ideas about him, has receded into the distance. There is no question in Job's mind that he is 'King' as we shall see, the one who is able to unleash the most awesome power and perform the most astounding miracles—but is he 'good'? That is the question found lingering on Job's lips. The avalanche of events which have fallen on this innocent man would seem to place a great question mark against answering that question in the affirmative. To pronounce, 'I believe in the greatness of God' is much easier than to declare 'I believe in the goodness of God.' From Job's perspective it is the Lord who in his sovereignty has given and taken away. But why? What possible reason could there be to lose the security of an income, the love of a family and the blessings of good health? What could justify the denigration of a man like Job as he moves from the status of an Arabian prince to a penniless pauper, sitting amongst the scavenging rats on the local dung heap (2:8)?

It has been suggested that one of the main questions which lies at the heart of the book; the problem which demands a resolution is found in verse 24 of chapter 9 and the rather ambiguous question: 'If it is not he [God], who then is it?'[2] As Job surveys not only the desolation in his own life, but some of the chaos which erupts in the natural order as well as the social upheavals in society, he asks this penetrating question. This question reveals the inner tension he is feeling, whilst at the same time reaches towards a possible solution.

Non-negotiable beliefs in tension

Job has two pillars of belief which uphold the edifice of his faith.

First, that God is sovereign over every twist and turn of existence—nothing can thwart him or surprise him, and so he rightly asks, 'If it is not he,' who is in some way behind such things, who else can it be?'

This brings into question the second pillar of his belief which is that God is righteous, for how can a good God have a hand in such things? In Job's mind it is difficult to see how the two can be reconciled, hence 2:10, 'Both good and bad come from God.' But how is this to be construed?

Job wants to affirm the sovereignty of God but finds it difficult to do so without attributing unrighteousness to him. We therefore have the other aspect of the ambiguous cry, 'If it is not he, then who is it?' Perhaps Job is vaguely entertaining the possibility that there is some other force or personality at work in the world, another 'who,' which is malevolent and wicked, although not a second god, for there is only one God. Therefore could it be that somehow God maintains both his sovereignty and goodness by permitting such a being to act whilst still achieving his righteous purposes, using this being as a kind of instrument? In some cases this will be as an agent in judging a wayward world—as if God were to say, 'If you refuse to have me as your loving ruler then there is always an alternative ruler.' Or it could be that sometimes this being becomes an instrument not so much to punish the wicked but to test the faithful, acting more like a fire to refine faith. Of course, we as the readers know from the first two chapters that such a creature exists, he is called the Satan. Although Job may be groping towards this idea, he doesn't quite grasp it, and so he continues to feel the inner anguish of wanting to hold on to the goodness of God in the face of suffering and evil.

No room for fatalism

In some ways this is a different Job from the one we

saw in chapter 3. There he was in a ditch out of which he couldn't climb. But now, to change the metaphor, Job is off the canvas and is ready to fight back. He may be knocked down but he isn't knocked out. Indeed, he is ready to hit back at his friends and wrestle with God. This is an important point.

Christian believers are not fatalists. They do not sit back, fold their arms and whatever comes their way simply mutter in pained resignation, 'Ah, it is the will of God.' Neither do they buy in to the theology of Doris Day, 'Que Sera, Sera—Whatever will be, will be.' No, Job has a razor sharp mind, he is a moral man with a deep sense of right and wrong, made in God's image and who can and will ask pertinent questions. There is that determined thinking through the issues so that he can come to some understanding of what is going on. He will push the question: 'If God is so good, why are things so bad?' And that is what God expects us to do, to use our minds within the limits of his revelation. This is 'faith seeking understanding.'

In chapter 9 Job responds to Bildad. In the previous chapter, Bildad has been arguing that God is always good and fair: 'Does God pervert justice? Or does the Almighty pervert the right?' (8:3) expecting the rhetorical answer 'of course not.' There is also the affirmation of 8:20, 'Behold, God will not reject a blameless man, nor take the hand of evildoers.' Job doesn't deny this as we see in 9:2a. 'Indeed, I know that this is true.' This is precisely part of the problem, if God does not pervert justice, why is it that prima facie he is allowing injustice to be worked out in Job's life? If God does not reject a blameless man, why does he appear to be rejecting this blameless man and especially his desire to be acquitted by God against all the slanderous accusations of his so called friends? Job is passionate to have access to the great Judge who is just so that he can be declared to be in the right.

Holding to integrity

What is at issue is his personal integrity. Had Job given in to the browbeating of his friends and lied in order to stop the suffering, saying, 'Yes I do deserve this,' then the Satan would have won his 'wager' for then Job would have shown that his own personal peace and prosperity mattered far more than true righteousness. John Walton describes Job's concern well when he writes, 'Job has called God's justice into question. Why does calling God's justice into question not constitute cursing God? The answer is to be found, I suggest, by investigating how and why he is questioning God's justice. Job does not doubt God's justice because he has lost his benefits, but rather because his own righteousness has been mitigated. His speeches have demonstrated that he cares little for restoration but greatly about righteousness.'[3]

But it appears that any possibility of being vindicated in the heavenly court is out of the question in 9:2–3: 'Truly I know that it is so: But how can a man be in the right before God? If one wished to contend with him, one could not answer him once in a thousand times.' Then again in vv.14–5: 'How then can I answer him, choosing my words with him? Though I am in the right, I cannot answer him; I must appeal for mercy to my accuser.'

Job wants an audience with God, but how? Even if he were to be admitted into the Divine presence he is scared stiff of the reception he might receive. Maybe you feel like that too. There are all sorts of questions you want to voice to God but you think that somehow God will disapprove of you if you did so and come down on you like some insecure head teacher for being impertinent. If so, then be encouraged to take a leaf out of Job's book and ask the questions which are on your heart with the Bible open before you.

What is happening?

There are three areas of life which Job looks at and asks: What is a good God doing? 'If it is not he, *who* is it?'

Nature disrupted

First, there is the area of nature. Here we are given a glimpse into the largeness of Job's view of God reflected in his overawed response to the glory of the universe God has made. The point is: if a cosmos is so great, then how much more the one who made it? Fittingly, Job employs the language of worship as we see in 9:5–10:

> … he who removes mountains, and they know it not, when he overturns them in his anger, who

shakes the earth out of its place, and its pillars tremble; who commands the sun, and it does not rise; who seals up the stars; who alone stretched out the heavens and trampled the waves of the sea; who made the Bear and Orion, the Pleiades and the chambers of the south; who does great things beyond searching out, and marvellous things beyond number.

This is no puny God Job serves. His litany of praise is not the soundbite of some of our choruses; it is the majestic language of the angels looking on in breathless wonder as God the great Artist sweeps his brush across the canvas of the heavens to produce galaxies, and whose voice thunders and mountains tremble. It therefore stands to reason that such a God would not be trivial in his dealings with the things he has made; he is a God who takes his creation and his creatures seriously. Therefore, there must be *some* reason for all that is happening, but what might that be?

Here we see through the eyes of Job that we live in a universe which has all the hallmarks of a cosmos—the well designed, intricate purposeful motions of planets, not the haphazard meanderings of rocks thrown up by Chance. If you think about it, it is the fact that we know we live in a world predominantly of order which causes us to believe that there is a God we can question when we come across the disorder. If the universe is at rock bottom ultimately random and meaningless with no rhyme or reason, people would not be asking the question: 'Why suffering?' It would be no more meaningful than asking 'Why dry rot?' It just 'is.'

We may think of it in this way. Suppose you want to lay a square patio of crazy paving in your garden you go ahead and order a load of broken flagstones. Once they have been delivered then there begins the tricky business of piecing them together. You will not be surprised in the least to discover that when you have finished you are left with a few pieces which can't be placed anywhere. You are not taken aback because you never thought that random, broken pieces were designed to fill up your square. It would not cross your mind to contact your supplier and complain that he didn't send the right type of flagstones for your garden!

Now imagine that you buy a jigsaw puzzle from a shop. You fit it all together carefully and thoughtfully, but at the end you are left with some pieces missing, more than that you have some pieces which do not even belong to your puzzle. Now you do have a right to be offended and complain. Why? Because underlying your complaint is the belief (rightly so) that there is intention, purpose and design behind the jigsaw puzzle, that is what makes a jigsaw puzzle different from crazy paving.

A similar situation exists when we come to the question of suffering. Suffering, we feel, doesn't quite fit in to the scheme of things. There would be no cause for complaint if underneath it all we didn't believe that the world was consciously designed by a good God.

Paradoxical though it may seem, the fact that we feel we have a right to complain is evidence that we really do believe there is a God to complain to, that our world is more like a well-designed jigsaw puzzle with some pieces missing rather than a pile of crazy paving we are expected to put together somehow.

Like us Job recognises that natural disasters occur, such as earthquakes, 'He shakes the earth from its place and makes its pillars tremble' (9:6), but God is still the one in control, he, as it were, does the shaking. Maybe something has happened which has caused some of the pieces of the 'jigsaw' to become dislocated. The Bible tells us there has—human sin. When the first man rebelled the whole of creation was ruptured. Sin has a dislocating effect and we are all affected. We shall be coming back to this in a later chapter, but suffice to say that the presence of evil in the world which is responsible for so much heartache, is represented here by the use of symbols for personal evil like the serpent in Genesis 3 and the Red Dragon in Revelation 13—the sea monster Rahab, v.13.[4] But note God is still the one who triumphs: 'beneath him bowed the helpers of Rahab.' Evil will not have the last say after all, God will.

When society falls apart

The second area of concern for Job is society. This is especially seen in 9:22–24:

> It is all one; therefore I say, 'He destroys both the blameless and the wicked.' When disaster brings

sudden death, he mocks at the calamity of the innocent. The earth is given into the hand of the wicked; he covers the faces of its judges—if it is not he, who then is it?

At least that is what it *seems* like.

Notice what an amazing man Job is. Even in the midst of all his problems he never becomes wholly self-consumed with the cry, 'Why me, me, me?' He has what today would be called a social conscience. He cares about others in society who seem to be denied justice. One of the reasons why God gave his law to his people Israel was so that order should reign in society as much as the solar system and act as a witness to his wisdom and righteousness (Deuteronomy 4:5–8). This sense of wholeness, harmony and well-being is described by the Bible writers as *shalom*. To receive God's shalom was to receive the highest blessing of all. If in some way there are forces of evil at work in the cosmos, then we would reasonably expect such forces to be at work in society to destroy the harmony God designates as good. Indeed, going back to Genesis 3, the shalom of the garden— that state of harmony between man and God, man and woman and man and nature—became disrupted when the lies of the serpent were listened to and the suggestion made that God was not good. Sadly, we have all been following suit ever since and reaping the consequences.

Justice is not always seen to be done in this world which is the contention of 9:22. 'It is all one; therefore I say, He destroys both the blameless and the wicked.' If justice is not done, then how can God be said to be just? Does it mean that evil men suffer the same fate as good men—both ending up in the grave—full stop? But if God *is* righteous, which Job still wants to believe is the case, and that he is all powerful, which he cannot deny, then might the fact that justice is denied in this life suggest the possibility that justice will be carried out in a future life? If so then God's justice and goodness would remain intact.

The sociologist, Peter Berger, observes how in the debate over the architect of Hitler's Jewish extermination programme, Adolf Eichmann, there was a general feeling that, 'hanging was not enough.' He points out that in the case of some human deeds no human punishment will ever be enough. In other words, there are deeds that demand not only human condemnation but divine damnation. It was Winston Churchill who once said that the evidence that 'God existed was the existence of Lenin and Trotsky, for whom hell was needed.'[5] That appears to be Job's sentiment too and it may well be yours. Later in chapter 19 Job, however dimly, glimpses the possibility that this might be so, that justice will be done and seen to be done and he will be there when it happens, 'For I know that my Redeemer [*go-el*—'Vindicator'] lives, and that at the last he will stand upon the earth [literally 'dust']. And after my skin has been thus destroyed, yet in my flesh I shall see God, whom I shall see for myself, and my eyes shall behold, and not another' (19:25–27). The reference to his skin being destroyed might mean that Job expects this experience to take place after his flesh has wasted away in death.

Of course Job has no developed belief of a resurrection, that comes later in the New Testament but the instinct is right. As we look at society with all its abuses, corruption and appalling evil, do we not long for one day when it will not only be removed but deservingly punished? This is not a thirst for vengeance but for justice—in Job's case vindication against the accusation of his friends. Without it God will cease to be God for he will have ceased to be just and that simply cannot be.[6]

Getting personal

There is also the chaos in Job's personal life. This is evident especially in the last three verses. 'If only there were someone to arbitrate between us, to lay his hand upon us both, someone to remove God's rod from me, so that his terror would frighten me no more. Then I would speak up without fear of him, but as it now stands with me, I cannot' (9:33–35 NIV). Like Susan in Narnia who is terrified at the prospect of meeting Aslan and yet desperate to see him, so it is with Job and God.

Although standing before God is seen as desirable in order that Job can plead his case, it is also seen as fearful, thus Job longs for someone who could arbitrate for him, some kind of go-between, a mediator who will act on his behalf in v.33 'If only there were someone to arbitrate between us.'[7] But here is the problem: who can approach God and live? Who can understand a man but a man? Is there anyone in the heavenly court who will speak for him? In short, is there an advocate?

As you read this there may be anguished longings in your soul. There is someone in your family who is causing your heart to ache, if not break. There are pressures on your mind which you long to unload. If only you could somehow reach out to God and speak to him knowing he will hear you and, perhaps more importantly, understand you because no one else seems to. But the gap feels too great and God too remote. If only there was someone who could reach down and put the hand of God into your hand and yours into his, someone who knows from the inside the anguish of a man like Job, who has been to the ash heap and triumphed and whose heart is tender towards us. The Gospel which Job anticipated and glimpsed from afar has come right into our midst—for that someone is Jesus. This is how the apostle John puts it in his first letter, 'we have an advocate with the Father, Jesus Christ the righteous. He is the propitiation for our sins.' The go-between is there, one mediator, one Lord, the God-man, Christ.

4 *Nearer the Truth*

Job 32-39

C.S. Lewis describes in agonising detail his wife's struggle with cancer in his *A Grief Observed*. At one point he writes, 'Not that I am (I think) in much danger of ceasing to believe in God. The real danger is in coming to believe such dreadful things about him. The conclusion I dread is not "so there is no God after all" but "so this is what God is really like. Deceive yourself no longer."'

We saw in the first chapter that one of the issues with which the Book of Job is concerned is 'How am I to think of God when I suffer?' This was precisely the question with which Job wrestled intensely. He couldn't deny God's existence any more than he could deny the existence of the sun, but he did begin to question God's character. Remember how he and his friends had bought into the retribution theory of justice—good is rewarded, evil is punished. Not surprisingly Job follows the reasoning through which this can be put in the form of a syllogism, with major premise, minor premise and conclusion: Suffering is punishment for wickedness (major premise); Job is innocent (minor premise); therefore God must be unjust (conclusion). This comes out in 27:2–5, 'As God lives, who has taken away my right, and the Almighty, who has made my soul bitter, as long as my breath is in me, and the spirit of God is in my nostrils, my lips will not speak falsehood, and my tongue will not utter deceit. Far be it from me to say that you are right; till I die I will not put away my integrity from me.' Elsewhere he cries, 'I loathe my life; I will give free utterance to my complaint; I will speak in the bitterness of my soul. I will say to God, Do not condemn me; let me know why you contend against me. Does it seem good to you to oppress, to despise the work of your hands …?' (10:1–3). Here Job is questioning God's righteousness, if good is rewarded and sin punished, as set out by the retribution theory, why then is he suffering so much when he is innocent? And that is when he comes perilously close to not denying God's existence but his goodness.

Stalemate

We have seen that the Book of Job is set out like a court room drama with accusation and defence going back and forth and appearing to end in stalemate. Job's friends who are the plaintiffs won't withdraw their case that it must be because Job is sinful that he suffers, and

Job the defendant refuses to agree with their assessment and points his finger in God's direction because he appears to be acting unjustly.

But there has been someone else present during the trial that has not yet been mentioned, Elihu who speaks in chapters 32–37.

A fresh voice

Elihu, unlike those of the other friends, has a Hebrew name meaning 'he is my God.' He has not spoken up to this point because he feels that as someone younger it is both wise and respectful to allow his elders to have their say first: 'I am young in years, and you are aged; therefore I was timid and afraid to declare my opinion to you' (32:6). Eventually he comes to the point where he can't hold back his anger any longer. He has listened to the three counsellors and to Job, and he finds them all to be found wanting in 32:12, 'I gave you my attention, and, behold, there was none among you who refuted Job or who answered his words.' Job has run rings around them until eventually they give up trying to argue. Instead they are reduced to adopting the attitude: 'We are right and you are wrong and that's that!'

But it is Job he has in his sights and spends the better part of five chapters rebuking him and defending God.

Opinions regarding Elihu vary. One writer calls Elihu 'an irascible, presumptuous blowhard.'[1] Others see him as being rather callous, lacking empathy with Job and his plight.[2] On the other hand, D.A. Carson, whilst recognising these defects, argues that Elihu is right to defend God's justice and warn Job of the danger of falling into the trap of exhibiting rebelliousness in his suffering.[3]

I would want to suggest that while there are some similarities between Elihu and Job's friends, in other significant ways he does stand apart from them and contributes an additional perspective on the role suffering might play in God's dealings with the world.

Whilst Elihu is younger than the others, his poetry is much more powerful and sophisticated than theirs, but of course not ascending to the heights of the Voice from the Whirlwind.[4] This is no mere upstart, there appears to be some measure of spiritual insight present.

Going too far

It is obvious that Job has incensed Elihu, not because of his protested innocence, but because he appears to be too eager to clear his own name at the expense of God's: 'Surely you have spoken in my ears, and I have heard the sound of your words. You say, "I am pure, without transgression; I am clean, and there is no iniquity in me. Behold, he finds occasions against me, he counts me as his enemy, he puts my feet in the stocks and watches all my paths." Behold, in this you are not right. I will answer you, for God is greater than man' (33:8–12).

Similarly in 34:12 we read: 'Of a truth, God will

not do wickedly, and the Almighty will not pervert justice.' In effect he is saying to Job, 'Look, you may well be as innocent as you say, and it will not do for your three friends to bring that into question; but by the same token it will not do for you to question God's righteousness. You may not have sinned so grossly when you started but you are coming pretty close to it now. You are wrong.'

There are basically two reasons Elihu gives as to why Job is going down the wrong path in his thinking and accusations against God to be acting unrighteously.

Know your limits

The first reason why Elihu believes Job to be misguided is because, 'God is greater than man' (33:12). Not simply that he is more powerful, but that his plans and purposes are on such a grand scale, far more complex and involved than our tiny minds can ever fully fathom. In the words of Isaiah 55:9, his ways are not our ways and his thoughts are higher than our thoughts. 'You see, Job,' says Elihu, 'your problem is that you are viewing God as if he were simply a man writ large, as if he were nothing but a capricious spiteful tyrant acting without reason. Just because *we* cannot immediately see what that reason is doesn't mean that there isn't one. God's timescale and concerns are much bigger than ours and we need to remember that.'

Purpose in pain

Secondly, following through this line of thought, Elihu suggests a different complementary perspective to understanding, in some measure, suffering. Instead of looking back for some cause and asking, 'Is this suffering due to Job's sin or God's injustice (when in fact it is neither)?' Elihu suggests that it might be more helpful to look forward to try and identify a purpose in suffering. In other words, if God is good and wise (and the supremacy of wisdom is celebrated in chapter 28 with a song), what we need to ask is, 'what possible good could there be in allowing suffering like this?'[5] The answer Elihu gives is that it is part of God's way of correcting us and preventing us from going off the rails entirely, as he puts it, it is that 'he may turn man aside from his deed and conceal pride from a man; he keeps back his soul from the pit' (33:17–18). In 33:19 he speaks of a man being 'rebuked with pain on his bed.' Later he claims that God makes people 'listen to correction and commands them to repent' (36:10) and 'speaks to them in their affliction' (36:15 NIV). Job has already complained that God has not spoken, but Elihu contends he is speaking 'now one way, now another' (33:14 NIV), that is, he is speaking to Job through suffering. Job's other friends insist that God should primarily be thought of as a judge, whereas Elihu suggests that the controlling model should be that of a teacher—'Who is a teacher like him?' (36:22). In other words, it is too narrow a view to think of all suffering as retribution; may it not be that some suffering is

God's instruction? Now we are getting very close to having some insight as to a purpose in this particular pain, for Elihu is not rebuked by God as are the other counsellors. Why? Perhaps because Elihu is near the mark in what he said. 'Here is a chastening use of suffering that may be independent of some particular sin. Its purpose may be preventative; it can stop a person from slithering down the slope to destruction.'[6]

A number of years ago I watched a television documentary series called *Commando*, about the training which goes into the making a Royal Marine. It was terrifying! You could imagine that a casual observer who knew nothing about what the instructors were trying to achieve would have drawn the conclusion that they simply hated the recruits. They would have seen the instructors physically hitting and yelling at these young men as they did a twenty-mile cross-country run with seventy pounds on their backs. Even if one of the recruits sprains an ankle or breaks a bone, it is nothing that a few painkillers can't put right and on they went! It all looked rather sadistic. But when the instructors explained what they were hoping to achieve, they said that they put these men through such a grilling regime in order to produce the best soldiers possible, knowing that their lives and the lives of others would depend upon that training. It was not retribution they were engaged in but instruction and character formation.

Suffering which shapes

This is how C.S. Lewis describes God's design in making us more the people he wants us to be so we see there is a purpose in pain: 'When a man turns to Christ and seems to be getting on pretty well (in the sense that some of his bad habits are now corrected) he often feels that it would now be natural if things went fairly smoothly. When troubles come along—illness, money troubles, new kinds of temptation he is disappointed. These things, he feels, might have been necessary to rouse him and make him repent in his bad old days; but why now? Because God is forcing him on, or up, to a higher level: putting him into situations where he will have to be very much braver, or more patient, or more loving, than he ever dreamed of being before. It seems to us all unnecessary: but that is because we have not yet had the slightest notion of the tremendous thing He means to make of us.'[7]

We have to admit that this is an idea which sits uncomfortably with many people today, including some Christians. We live in a culture where pleasure is prized above all else and where pain is to be avoided at all costs. We expect that everything should come to us with maximum ease and minimum discomfort, producing what some have dubbed 'the snowflake generation.' Some Christians also expect life to be easy. The idea that something, such as having a personal relationship with God, might be so valuable that it is worth undergoing some trouble to get it, grates with many in the church, both young and old. Why bother coming to church every Sunday, why bother with the hard graft of Bible study or listening to a sermon, why put up with the discipline of prayer or finding ways of serving God which costs in terms of time and effort? We may not always voice it that way but, as we look around many of our churches today, that is the message coming across loud and clear. A number of years ago, Dr Leon Morris pinpointed the problem: 'True worship is at a cost. This is something that still needs to be learned on a day when men and women take churchgoing lightly, when they will go to church only if it is easy, if the church is near, if the choir is good, if the preacher is approved, if the weather isn't bad, if friends haven't dropped in for a visit, and if a 101 other things haven't stopped them. If worship means a real effort, then men and women today are often disinclined to make it.' In this kind of cultural climate we can expect God all the more to shake us out of our complacency and pride by putting us through the mill. We may think of it this way: God doesn't want spoilt little brats who think that he owes them a favour, rather he wants loving obedient children who will trust him come what may

The question is: how will we respond?

We can be like sulky children, locking ourselves away in our room, building up resentment towards God for the way he is treating us, refusing to open the door in response to his knocking. God gives us that choice. Elihu warns Job that he is in danger of allowing this to happen to him: 'Take care; do not turn to iniquity, for this you have chosen rather than affliction' (36:21).

Or we can be like trusting children who, while expressing the hurt and the pain, even raising their voice in perplexity, 'Why Lord?', nevertheless in the midst of difficulty will ask, 'Father, what are you teaching me through this, what might I learn?'

One way by which the faith not only of an individual can be refined but whole churches is through persecution. Writing of her experience in the dark days of the Soviet Union when many Christians were imprisoned for their faith, one Russian believer said: 'My first fifteen-day sentence taught me a great deal about myself. In such a situation you see your good points and bad points very clearly. You find out where your weaknesses are. Persecution can be compared to a photographic developer. When the film is immersed in the developer, an image appears. When a Christian encounters persecution, his character becomes evident. Our church quickly learned who was ready for persecution and who wasn't.'[8]

The point Elihu is making is that this is what might be happening with Job, at least in part. Elihu is defending the righteousness of God and that whilst Job had not necessarily displayed sin in anything he had done before this suffering came upon him, there is a danger that he is displaying rebellion in suffering by impugning God's character. We are back to the question we began with: 'What kind of God will we believe in in the midst of suffering?'

The three horns

The problem believers face has been put in the form of a trilemma which was originally formulated by the Greek philosopher Epicurus: 'Is God willing to prevent evil, but not able? Then he is impotent. Is he able but not willing? Then he is malevolent. Is he both able and willing? Whence evil?' Or, as stated more recently by John Hick: 'If God is perfectly loving and good he must wish to abolish evil; if God is all powerful he must be able to abolish evil. But evil exists therefore God cannot be both perfectly good and almighty.'[9]

Several attempts have been made to solve this conundrum, which in some way or other involve the denial of one of those elements which makes up the trilemma in the first place.

Some would deny that God is all powerful, severely revising ideas about his omnipotence and omniscience. I remember attending a clergy conference where a deaconess passionately argued for what she called 'a weak God.' She was adamant that it gave her comfort to think that God was busy struggling with life and getting it wrong just like the rest of us. In a more sophisticated form this is the position of those who advocate 'Open Theism.' There are those of this school who argue that God can't know what will happen in the future, but is only aware of the various possibilities of what might happen, this, it is claimed, preserves God's goodness, for if he knows evil will happen and does not take steps to prevent it, then he shares in its responsibility.[10]

On the other hand, there are those who would deny the existence of suffering viewing it as 'illusory' in some way. For example, Theravada Buddhism considers suffering (*dukkha*) as part of 'Maya'—belonging to the vale of illusion. Similarly with Christian Science which views 'pain' to be a product of 'the mortal mind.' But this is hardly satisfactory for most people undergoing hardship. One is reminded of the limerick:

> There was once a faith healer from Deal
> who said although pain is not real,
> when I sit on a pin and I puncture my skin,
> I dislike what I imagine I feel!

Can we honestly say that suffering is not a reality?

There would be others still who would want to question God's goodness, especially his justice. This was the cry of the French philosopher Baudelaire who exclaimed, 'If there is a God, he is the very devil.' This is the theme running through Archibald MacLeish's play, *J.B.*, an updated re-presentation of the story of Job. At various intervals throughout the play there is the haunting refrain, 'If he is God he is not good, if he is good he is not God.' In the play a clergyman tells J.B. that his suffering is caused by the simple fact he is a man, that it is all part of the human condition, to which J.B. responds, 'Yours is the cruellest comfort of all, making the Creator of the Universe the miscreator of mankind, a party to the crimes He punishes.'[11]

Whilst not going that far, Job certainly found himself struggling with the idea that God was just, given what he was suffering. Job knew God was all powerful, Job certainly knew evil and suffering existed, but what of God's goodness? This is what he came close to denying and which Elihu seeks to correct by saying, 'those who suffer [God] delivers in [lit. through] their suffering; he speaks to them in their affliction. He is wooing you from the jaws of distress to a spacious place free from restriction, to the comfort of your table laden with choice food' (36:15–16 NIV). The call of Elihu is, 'Be patient; it is better to be a chastened saint than a carefree sinner.'[12]

Patience in pain

What might such patience look like which holds fast to the sovereignty and goodness of God in the midst of suffering?

Perhaps something like what happened to Jerry Sittser.

In 1991 a drunk driver veered across the road into the car of Jerry Sittser and his family. His mother, wife and daughter were all killed—three generations in one moment. His book, *A Grief Disguised*, is a painfully honest reflection on his story. Yet Sittser writes: 'It is possible to live in and be enlarged by loss, even as we continue to experience it.' He continues: 'Sometimes

I wonder about how my own experience of loss will someday serve a greater purpose that I do not yet see or understand. My story may help to redeem a bad past, or future. Perhaps my own family heritage has produced generations of absent and selfish fathers, and I have been given a chance to reverse that pattern. Perhaps people suffering catastrophic loss will someday look to our family for hope and inspiration. I do not know. Yet I choose to believe that God is working towards some ultimate purpose, even using my loss to that end.'[13]

It is sometimes the case that it is not so much our situation but the way we react to that situation which makes all the difference in handling suffering. This was a point made by the late David Watson, 'A little time ago I talked with two young fathers within a period of about four months. Both had tragically lost their children of four or five. One had died of leukaemia; the other had been drowned in a swimming pool. One father had been a professing Christian but was now, through the experience, a militant atheist. The other father had been a humanist and was now, through the experience, almost a Christian. Here were two very similar tragic experiences but with totally different reactions.' Watson goes on to write, 'These reactions are tremendously important. If I become bitter and resentful through my suffering, I still have my suffering, but on top of that I have to contend with my bitterness and resentment as well; and this may be even worse than my initial suffering. Certainly it would be worse for other people, and I am responsible for that. On the other hand, if in my suffering I open my heart to the love and peace and friendship of Jesus Christ, then this will wonderfully transform the entire situation—a fact which I see in pastoral work virtually every week of my life.'[14]

Be careful

Perhaps, however, in the case of Job the idea being put forward by Elihu of the instructional nature of suffering needs to be applied with some care and modified slightly. Suffering can be a means of moral instruction (the 'megaphone of pain' to use C.S. Lewis's celebrated phrase) and so character cleansing. But is that the main concern with Job who is praised by God as there being 'none like him' a phrase more often used in the Bible of God himself (Psalm 86:8)? John Piper thinks it is:

I picture Job as a beaker of water. Job had been so worked upon by the grace of God that his life was pure. You could see right through the water. People looked at him and they saw a pure man. But there was a sediment of self-reliance and pride at the bottom. It wasn't huge and it wasn't damning, but it was there. When God shook Job, the sediment coloured the water, and you find Job saying some terrible things about God in this book. God knew that it was there, and he knew that in shaking this godly, blameless man there would arise some imperfection into his life, and that it would need to be purged. So the last thing is, therefore, 'I despise myself, and repent in dust and ashes.'[15]

Whilst not ruling out entirely that some refining of Job took place (and surely anyone going through such an experience and still coming out trusting in God would have a stronger faith than at the beginning and would have engaged in some self-examination), perhaps the 'instructing' element of suffering should be thought of less as addressing a moral defect than as deepening a spiritual perspective. In that sense the notion of God being a teacher, as advocated by Elihu, still applies, but in a more subtle way.

While in my opinion he may go too far in playing down the refining purpose of suffering along the lines enunciated by Elihu, Eric Ortland does make an important point when he writes, 'It appears that we need a third category of suffering. Sometimes God allows pain and loss that have nothing to do with sin in our lives and are not meant to teach us anything. Rather, our loss and bewilderment becomes an avenue by which God gives himself to us more than he ever could have before, when we were at ease (29:6). When God puts us into a position where we must hold onto our relationship with God for God's sake only—in which we stand to gain nothing but God—we start to receive him more fully than we ever had before. Job's amazed cry, 'Now my eyes see you,' becomes our own.[16]

God is the reward.

5 *A Voice from the Storm*

Job 38–41

IN 1949 C.S. LEWIS WROTE AN ESSAY ENTITLED *GOD IN the Dock*. In it he says that one of the main differences between an earlier generation of seekers of God and those of the present day is that there used to be a fair degree of humility because people had a sense of approaching someone infinitely greater than themselves. That has all changed. He writes, 'The ancient man approached God (or even the gods) as the accused person approaches his judge. For the modern man the roles have been reversed. He is the judge: God is in the dock. He is quite a kindly judge: if God should have a reasonable defence for being the God who permits war, poverty and disease, he is ready to listen to it. The trial may even end in God's acquittal. But the important thing is that man is on the bench and God is in the dock.'[1]

In many respects what Lewis said is true. But interestingly enough the Book of Job provides an exception, because here we see God, as it were, being put in the dock by Job himself. 'At the beginning of the book it looks as though Job is on trial ... But in terms of the development of the book, it is clear that it is God who is on trial; suffering and evil are merely pointers towards the greatest problem of all, namely, God!'[2]

A cry for justice

It is obvious that Job is more than indignant about his situation of abject misery and the cutting accusations of his three counsellors that somehow he is the guilty one. He wants God to vindicate him (19:25—a 'redeemer' *go-el*—vindicator) and if that is at the expense of God's name then so be it. This is not hard to understand. Listen, for example, to the cries of three women: 'I am falsely accused.' 'If it was the last moment to live, God knows I am innocent.' 'I am wronged. It is a shameful thing that you should mind these folks that are out of their wits.' Those were the anguished appeals of Sarah Good, Elizabeth Howe, and Martha Carrier which fell on deaf hears before they were hanged at the Salem witch trials in New England in 1692.[3] As such they stand as a haunting reminder that few things in life are more terrible than to be falsely accused with no one around to defend you. That was Job's feeling too.

But Job is not solely concerned about his own plight but also that of others. He asks, 'Why do the wicked live, reach old age, and grow mighty in power?' (21:7); 'Why are not times of judgment kept by the Almighty, and why do those who know him never see his days?' (24:1) In other words why do the guilty seem to get off 'scot free' and those who are faithful suffer for their faithfulness?

The case against God

We have seen that the drama of the book is set out like a courtroom which can be thought of as a triangle made up of three protagonists. There are Job's friends who are accusing Job of wrongdoing which they see is the explanation for his suffering. There is God who is being accused by Satan for setting up a faulty system of rewards a n d

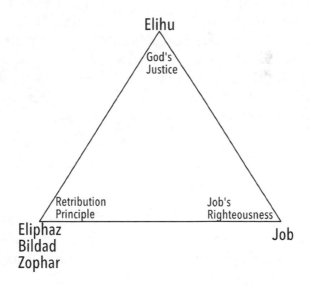

punishments and Job who also feels that God is not
behaving as he should. There is also young Elihu who
stands in God's corner to defend his just character.[4]

If God is in the dock, as he is in the minds of many
people today and in the mind of Job and the Satan,
then what must happen for God to lose his case that he
has not set up a flawed system of morality, but that it is
possible for people to do good for its own sake without
any thought of personal gain? The quickest way would
be for Job to take the advice of his wife, 'Curse God and
die' (2:9), for then the Satan would have been right; Job
was in the 'God business' only for what he could get out
of it. It is sad to say that there are those who profess to
be Christian believers who take that same attitude. They
are only committed to their religion so long as they have
a good job, good health, nice family and a thousand and
one other things which make life pleasant. Dare God
take away any of these, he touches the apple of their eye
and soon becomes an object of disdain. Of course, what
they are worshipping is a false god, a sugar-daddy god,
who is no god at all. And so maybe the sooner that is
exposed the better.

The second way God could be shown to be failing is
by Job following the advice of his friends in trying to
appease God. This springs from a false view that God is
unprincipled and capricious like some drunken abusive
father; you just never know when he is going to explode
in a bad temper so you are always walking on eggshells,
forever anxiously trying to placate him. But had Job

gone along with this, then Satan's charge would have held: Job was only interested in himself and not truth or justice. Those are Satan's charges, which don't stick, because Job doesn't give in; he really is righteous and God is vindicated in the choice of his servant.

But what of Job's charge against God being unjust? This would hold if the retribution principle were to remain unmodified. This is where the argument of Elihu comes into its own that some hard things come our way not in order to punish us but to instruct us, perhaps getting us to change our priorities and checking spiritual drift. It is obvious that the world doesn't operate in terms of strict cause-and-effect because we can see that many a good person has suffered terribly while many a tyrant has died peacefully in their sleep surrounded by fame and fortune (21:17). So might it not be that things are rather more complicated in the world and that bad things do happen to good people?

Job remains insistent that God appears and defends himself, and seems to take God's silence as a sign that he has surrendered to Job's accusations, 31:35 NIV, 'Oh, that I had someone to hear me! I sign now my defence—let the Almighty answer me; let my accuser put his indictment in writing' (31:33 NIV). With the possible implication he hasn't because he can't.

However, God eventually does appear and speaks but not quite as Job had hoped, he speaks out of the whirlwind: 'Who is this that darkens counsel by words without knowledge?' (38:2). As G.K. Chesterton writes,

'He [God] is quite willing to be prosecuted. He only asks for the right which every prosecuted person possesses; He asks to be allowed to cross-examine the witness for the prosecution.'[5]

Divine encounter

God bombards Job with some eighty rhetorical questions. There are three types of questions: first, *who* questions, which point to God's power, for example, in 38:28, 'who has begotten the drops of dew?' Secondly, *what* questions, which emphasises Job's complete inability, such as in 39:27, 'Is it at *your* command that the eagle mounts up and makes his nest on high?' Thirdly, there are the *have you ever* questions reinforcing the limits of human knowledge—'Can you bring forth the constellations?' (38:32).[6]

At the outset of this close encounter of the Divine kind we see a massive change of pace as the poetry of God outstrips everyone else's, showing that God is taking things to an entirely new level:

Then the LORD answered Job out of the whirlwind and said: "Who is this that darkens counsel by words without knowledge? Dress for action like a man; I will question you, and you make it known to me. Where were you when I laid the foundation of the earth? Tell me, if you have understanding. ... Have you commanded the morning since your days began, and caused the dawn to know its place? ... Have you entered the storehouses of the snow, or have you seen the storehouses of the hail, which I have reserved for the time of trouble? ... Can you bind the chains of the Pleiades or loose the cords of Orion? Can you lead forth the constellations in their season?" (38:4–5, 12, 22, 31–32).

Job is barraged with question after question (38:39–39:30): 'What about the animals? Do you provide for them, Job? Have you got so great a mind that out of nothing you could come up with such a strange looking bird as an ostrich? You think you are so wise, Job, and I am so useless!' Job had wanted an interview with the Almighty, and that is precisely what he got but perhaps not in the way he expected.

We come to the heart of God's concern with Job in 40:8–14:

Will you even put me in the wrong? Will you condemn me that you may be in the right? Have you an arm like God, and can you thunder with a voice like his? Adorn yourself with majesty and dignity; clothe yourself with glory and splendour. Pour out the overflowings of your anger, and look on everyone who is proud and abase him. Look on everyone who is proud and bring him low and tread down the wicked where they stand. Hide them all in the dust together; bind their faces in the world below. Then will I also acknowledge to you that your own right hand can save you.

It's as if God is saying: 'Just who do you think you

are Job? To protest your innocence is one thing, but to accuse me of injustice is another. In order to make the right judgment upon me and what I am doing you have to have a lot more wisdom and knowledge than you have. You have not been able to answer a single one of my questions Job, questions to which I have all the answers. Does it not therefore occur to you that I just might have the answer as to why I permit suffering? If you cannot comprehend the intricacies of the creation which you can see, then can you honestly expect to grasp the mysteries of the spiritual realm which you can't see? Only I, God, can do that which includes the mystery of suffering.' 'In other words, God does not here answer Job's questions about the problem of evil and suffering, but *he makes it unambiguously clear what answers are not acceptable in God's universe.*'7

Distorted vision

However, it would be a mistake to see God's speech against Job simply to be one of harsh rebuke and a call to recognise the limits of his own creatureliness, although it is no less than that. Remember how, in chapter 9, Job drew attention to the chaos in the cosmos, the dis-order amongst the order, trying to gain some understanding of why this should be so and permitted by God? Could it be that in his pain Job has fallen into such a dark abyss that he no longer sees the sun and his perspective on reality becomes distorted? It is this wrong way of viewing things which God also corrects which will eventually lead to an enlarging of Job's vision of

God and the deepening of his faith. Ortland describes this process well:

In 38:4–7, for instance, YHWH describes the founding of the earth in a way that counters Job's conviction that God destroys the good order of creation by shaking the earth out of its foundations (9:6) and that the earth is under the control of the worst sort of people (9:24). Job has, understandably but wrongly, pulled into himself in his pain, viewing everything through the lens of his tragedy. In his eyes, the world is a sinister, chaotic mess. God expands Job's vision to show him beings higher than himself unable to restrain their praise (38:7) as God establishes the very place Job has "darkened." Similarly, 38:12–15 shows the moral edge to creation. The poetry is complex, but the description of the rising sun chasing the wicked away (v. 13) and breaking their arm (a symbol for strength, v. 15) implies that there is a moral edge to the architecture of creation. The order of creation resists evil—a very different perspective from Job's in his protest. The description of the sea in 38:8–11 is especially striking in that it activates one of the most powerful biblical symbols for chaos and evil (cf. Psalm 18:5–6, Habakkuk 3:15, Revelation 21:1). Most often in OT poetry, YHWH wages war against the chaotic watery powers (e.g., Job 7:12, 26:11–13). Here, he treats the sea like an infant as he diapers it (v. 9), even though it is still resisting him! That is the meaning of the reference in v. 11 to the "proud waves" of the sea—

even though it does not submit to him, YHWH still cares for this part of his creation as he restricts and contains it. YHWH is communicating to his scarred servant that he does allow some chaotic and sinister elements in his creation (such as the predators of 39:26–30), but only within strict limits (vv.8,10)—and he is far gentler and kinder even with chaos than Job has imagined. Creation is a good place in which God delights, not an amoral jungle ruled by an arbitrary tyrant, as Job had imagined.[8]

God's defence wasn't quite as Job anticipated. At the first pause Job answers: 'Behold, I am of small account [literally 'I am humbled']; what shall I answer you? I lay my hand on my mouth' (40:4). The way litigation was carried out in an ancient Jewish court was not for someone involved in a lawsuit to convince the judge or jury of his innocence, but his accuser, so that the plaintiff would withdraw his accusation and acknowledge defeat by placing his hand over his mouth. That is what happened to Job, his case for the prosecution collapses like a stack of cards.

We might also ask: why should we presume that God owes us an explanation of why he allows suffering, any more than he owes us an explanation of why he made the ostrich the way he did? It may be true that whilst we can't see why he should design so peculiar a bird, no doubt God had plenty of good reasons for doing so, if only known to himself. Could not the same be said for suffering? In other words, if there is a fair degree of mystery when it comes to trying to understand the workings of an ordered universe, how much more so when it comes to trying to understand suffering in a broken universe?

More to the point, is it not reasonable to trust a God who has both the wisdom and the power to create so mind-boggling a universe, even if we may not be able to understand all the whys and wherefores of what happens in it?

God cares

What is also striking of God's defence of his ways is not simply an appeal to Divine power, but Divine care, what Eleanor Stump has even dubbed the 'maternal care' of his creation, 'Can you hunt the prey for the lion, or satisfy the appetite of the young lions, when they crouch in their dens or lie in wait in their thicket? Who provides for the raven its prey, when its young ones cry to God for help, and wander about for lack of food?' (38:39–41)

Stump writes, 'If an innocent person suffers, then, it will be because a good God, a loving God involved face-to-face with his creatures, produces out of his suffering a good meant for that person which in the circumstances couldn't have been produced or produced as well, without the suffering. The inference to this explanation about suffering is available to Job ... In addition, however, Job has another source of information about God's reasons for allowing him to suffer ... It is the experience of God which he has while God is talking to him.'9

Knowing that we don't know

Job finally realised his mistake, which is often ours, namely, to think that we are privy to all the facts, when we are not; we are under the illusion that we can 'out god God' and maybe secretly think that if we were God we would do a much better job of things. However, even if we were to have all the facts available we would not be able to put them together in such a way that they would make complete sense. Our minds are too tiny for that. Or even if we think we have a handle on most of the facts we are then tempted to be reductionistic in our understanding of how the facts are to be pieced together and interpreted and so come up with something like the retribution principle which the Book of Job has shown to be found singularly lacking.

What is pivotal is that Job's mistake turns out to be the mirror image of that of his faithless friends, though for a better reason. All of them err by starting from the faulty one-to-one accounting of sin and suffering that was common at the time. This false accounting leads Job's friends to an equally false accusation: Job is suffering, so he must have sinned. They have no idea of the unseen dimensions of the contest ... On the other hand; this false accounting leads Job to a false demand for a one-to-one explanation from God. He has no idea of the unseen dimensions either, so to defend himself from what he knows to be false—"I am not what you think me to be"—Job demands from God a one-to-one explanation of his suffering. And when he does not get it, he dares to try to clear his own name by accusing God himself of injustice, not knowing either God or what really is at stake in the story.[10]

Realising his error and humbled by his encounter Job's response is not to rise up in arrogance and persist in his demand that God explains everything, but rather to repent of presumption and fall down in worship:

> Then Job answered the LORD and said: "I know that you can do all things, and that no purpose of yours can be thwarted. 'Who is this that hides counsel without knowledge?' Therefore I have uttered what I did not understand, things too wonderful for me, which I did not know. 'Hear, and I will speak; I will question you, and you make it known to me.' I had heard of you by the hearing of the ear, but now my eye sees you; therefore I despise myself, and repent in dust and ashes." (42:1–6)

Cultural challenge

The Book of Job challenges our present culture at two decisive points.

First, it confronts our man-centred understanding of our place in the universe. Daniel J. Estes correctly observes that, 'In many ways, the contemporary *Zeitgeist* finds the book of Job perplexing and even offensive. For those who accept the prevalent narcissism of the age, assuming that "it is all about me," Job counters instead that life is all about God and his order for the world. People today place great faith in science and technology, confident that there must be answers to their questions if only humans would search hard enough. Job, by contrast, challenges the reader to accept that the Lord has knowledge that surpasses what humans can know, so that we must accept mystery and place our faith in the God who knows far more than he has revealed.'[11] It goes against the grain of fallen human nature to consider that there is Another greater than itself who occupies a position higher than itself. The Book of Job shows how pitiful and shallow people's normal understanding is.

Secondly, it tarnishes one of the major jewels in the crown of 'modernity' that with the right use of reason there is nothing that cannot be conquered. Job's challenge is to live within the limits of reason. Reason and rationality can take us only so far—and often very far—for example, consider the success of modern science. But the error we make is in thinking that a method which has been so successful in one sphere (science) can be transferred and applied to another sphere (theology) with the same expected measure of success. But the devastating effects of 19th century and early 20th century theological liberalism which tried to apply 'scientific methodology' has shown that to be a false expectation.[12] 'Do not seek to know more than is appropriate' wrote Augustine of Hippo. This was a sentiment echoed many centuries later by Blaise Pascal in his *Pensees*, 'Let us then know our reach. We are something and not everything ... Our intelligence occupies in the order of things the same place as our body in the extent of nature.' Both statements act as succinct summaries of one of the lessons Job had to learn and post-Enlightenment man still needs to learn.

However, whilst using reason is certainly one way of knowing it is not the only way. Plantinga rightly notes, 'when God does come to Job in the whirlwind, it is not to convince him that God really does have reasons (although it may, in fact, do this); it is instead to still the tempest in his soul, to quiet him, to restore his trust for God. The Lord gives Job a glimpse of his greatness, his beauty, his splendid goodness, the doubts and turmoil disappear and are replaced once more, by love and trust.'[13] Job's mind has not been bypassed, if anything, by this Socratic questioning of God, it has been expanded, but what has been further addressed through his mind is his heart.[14]

John Piper eloquently distinguishes the 'knowledge' of Job's three friends, that of Elihu and the personal knowledge finally embraced by Job, 'Neither bad theology (in the words of Eliphaz, Bildad, and Zophar) nor good theology (in the words of Elihu) gives us the knowledge of God which changes a person's heart. "Taste and see that the LORD is good!" (Psalm 34:8). There is a knowledge that only comes through tasting. Five seconds of honey on the tongue will show you more sweetness than ten hours of lectures about the sweetness of honey. "Taste and see that the LORD is good." Until God gives you a taste of his goodness all the theology in the world will not give you a knowledge of his goodness that changes your heart and saves your soul.'[15]

A number of years ago I found myself in the middle of a spiritual whirlwind in which I was under immense pressure, feeling not a little disorientated under its assault. But what I also found was that in this moment of trial God became so real; the Bible seemed to change from black and white to colour and some of its passages had such a sense of immediacy there was no doubting God's voice and comfort—it was almost audible. I had known many of these passages before, together with their theological meaning and application. But in the suffering they almost took on a life of their own, a depth and texture I would not have known apart from the suffering which they addressed. This is the different kind of 'knowing' alluded to by Plantinga and Stump and discovered by Job.

The encounter of Job with God has been summarised well by Bartholomew and O'Dowd: 'While the divine speeches make Job's finitude clear, their focus is on Yahweh's power and wisdom in creating and ruling his world. Job is as much rebuked as, together with the characters and the audience, called to a new wisdom of trust and even wonder—a discipline of humility and faith in the midst of mystery and suffering that returns again and again to God's ability to rule his world justly and lovingly.'[16]

Our God is too small

Suffering and evil are problems to us as they were to Job not because God is too small and struggling like the rest of us (the error of Open Theism), but because he is so great that we cannot fathom what he is doing. Or in the words of an old Portuguese proverb, 'God writes straight with crooked lines.' There is meaning in it all somewhere (God *is* writing straight) but with 'crooked lines' (and so we find them difficult to read).

At the end of it all there are only two corners of the 'triangle' left. God *is* just and Job *is* righteous and the retribution principle does not hold true in every situation and certainly not in this case. His friends were wrong about God and Job and it is they who are in the dock, as we shall see.

This is what we are left with:

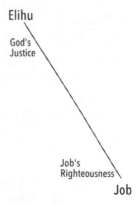

What God really wants

However, it may be that you still feel sceptical that having gone through all the trials and questioning, a humble worshipful submission is really possible. You may think that while such a posture can be concocted at the literary level with a book like Job, in real life it isn't quite like that. I sympathise with you if that is your view. But God *has* furnished us with many examples of people whose faith having been forged on the anvil of pain have come to know God as almighty, all loving and all wise, whilst resting content with what they didn't know. One such man was George Mueller.

Together with his wife, Mary, he set up the Ashley Down orphanage in Bristol and during the course of their lives cared for over 10,000 children. They also established 117 schools which offered Christian education to more than 120,000 children, many of whom were orphans.

It is almost beyond our comprehension to think of how God used such a couple for the benefit of so many as they exercised their simple faith in him. It was a faith tested many times, but the greatest test came with the death of Mueller's wife of thirty four years to rheumatic fever. Having been through so much together with so much more yet to do, was it possible for Mueller to rest in God's wisdom?

Mueller preached at her funeral laying out three points, his third being, 'The Lord was good and did good in taking her from me.' Under this point he related how he had prayed for her during her illness, 'Yes, my Father, the times of my darling wife are in Thy hands. Thou wilt do the very best thing for her and for me, whether life or death. If it may be, raise up yet again my precious wife, Thou art able to do it, though she is so ill; but whatsoever Thou dealest with me, only help me to continue to be perfectly satisfied with thy Holy will.' Then looking back on the way God responded to this prayer he said, 'Every day I see more and more how great is her loss to the orphans. Yet, without an effort, my inmost soul habitually joys in the joy of that loved departed one. Her happiness gives joy to me. My dear daughter and I would not have her back, were it possible to produce it by the turn of a hand. God himself has done it; we are satisfied with Him.'

The example of Mueller illustrates beautifully the lesson of Job described by Ortlund, 'When we find ourselves in Job-like suffering, what God wants from us is not complicated: we are to hold on to our relationship with him and not give up on him.'[17] The wonderful thing is that God did not give up on Job as he will not give up on all who are bound by his covenant love in Jesus.

6 *The Unmasking of Evil*

Job 40–41

THE HIPPOPOTAMUS MAY SEEM TO US TO BE A RATHER comical creature thanks largely to Walt Disney and Flanders and Swann; but the fact is that it is quite a fearsome beast which accounts for many deaths in Africa each year. Some argue that the animal referred to as 'Behemoth' in Job 40:15 is just that—a hippo and that the Leviathan in 41:1 is a crocodile.[1] If that is so, it does seem to be a strange argument that God is using in response to Job's complaint about suffering in the world in general and his own suffering in particular.

In his book, *War in Heaven*, the friend of C.S. Lewis, Charles Williams, describes a conversation between a sceptic, called Mornington and an Archdeacon: 'As a mere argument there's something lacking perhaps, in saying to a man who's lost his money and his house and his family and is sitting on the dustbin, all over boils, "Look at the hippopotamus." "Job seemed to be impressed," the Archdeacon said mildly. "Yes," Mornington admitted. "He was certainly the perfect fool, in one meaning or other of the words.'" George Bernard Shaw cynically insisted 'that God, when challenged about his justice and providence, really needs to do better than retort: "You can't make a hippopotamus can you?"'

If that is all the Behemoth and Leviathan are—hippos and crocodiles—then it has to be admitted that it doesn't make for a convincing argument in the face of human suffering, it seems a non sequitur. But what if they are more than they appear at first sight? Since ten verses are given over to describing the Behemoth and thirty-four verses to the Leviathan this might suggest there is more to them than meets the eye. I hope to show that is the case, that through these two creatures we are being introduced to a supernatural world, a world which involves one very significant supernatural creature behind much of the suffering, death and all of the evil which has been in evidence during the earth's long history.[2]

Symbols with significance

We all know how animals can represent peoples or a person. Think of the British bulldog, a symbol of strength and determination. Or consider how C.S. Lewis drew on the imagery of a Lion, Aslan, to represent Christ in the *Chronicles of Narnia*. Similarly the ancients used images to depict things, not least forces of evil and chaos. For example, there is the ancient Egyptian story of Seti, the god of darkness who took the form of a hippopotamus to battle the god of light, Horus.[3] If that kind of imagery was in circulation in the ancient world, we shouldn't be so surprised that similar imagery is taken by the biblical writers not to speak of mythical gods, but actual beings who stand in opposition to the true God.[4]

First, let's think about the identity of the creatures.

Describing death

There is the Behemoth. This is the plural form of a common Hebrew word simply meaning 'beast.' So what we might have being spoken of here is the Beast *par excellence*. One of the most disturbing novels written in the mid-20th century is *Lord of the Flies*. The author, William Golding, wrote that story following the horrors of World War Two partly to explain why human beings are capable of such appalling evil. In the story a group of public school boys marooned on a desert island degenerate into savages. At the centre is the Beast, a sinister figure which is both the evil inside the boys and a pigs head on a stick. The pig's head embodies the evil surging through the veins of the boys. Perhaps we have something similar going on here with Behemoth.

On the one hand, whatever it is it's still a creature made by God alongside all other creatures, for example, v.15, 'Look at Behemoth, which I made along with you and which feeds on grass like an ox.' But on the other hand, there is something decidedly sinister and intimidating about it, so verse 19a could be rendered, 'Let him that made him keep his sword unsheathed!'[5] In other words, even God has to be especially wary with this one!

Given that chapter 39 ends with cruelty and death, and in verse 13 of chapter 40 God challenges Job about death, 'Bury them all in the dust together; shroud their faces in the grave.' It seems likely that Behemoth symbolises death itself as a giant creature which is able to bring about death and over which no human being can prevail, 'Can anyone capture it by the eyes, or trap it and pierce its nose?' (40:24), to which the expected answer is 'no.' But we know from the New Testament that there is one, Jesus, who has conquered death, the very thing which has held human beings captive and, more to the point, he has defeated the one who holds the power of death itself—Satan (Hebrews 2:14–15).

The problem with Job's friends (and to some extent with Job himself) is that their view of the world doesn't have much room for a creature like Behemoth which brings disorder, chaos and death. Their world is too neat and tidy, operating in a strict relationship of cause and effect—good is rewarded, wickedness punished. But if there is some malevolent spiritual being at work upsetting that order then they need to think again. Perhaps here God is getting Job to consider such an idea by drawing on imagery which exists in the surrounding cultures representing this reality.

Taking off the mask

However, it is when we turn to the next creature in chapter 41 that the unmasking of evil becomes more apparent.

One good rule to apply when trying to get to grips with a more baffling part of Scripture is to turn to other clearer parts of Scripture for light.

We need to ask: where else does the 'Leviathan' appear in the Bible?

In the first place, it surfaces at different points in the story of Job itself. The first appearance occurs in chapter 3:8 which follows on from Satan's disappearance in chapter 2:3, 'May the day of my birth perish, [says Job] and the night it was said, 'A boy is born!' May those who curse days curse that day, those who are ready to rouse Leviathan.' Here the monster is, like Behemoth, associated with death. This is a 'grim reaper' figure.

Another name given to this sea monster is 'Rahab' which in chapter 9:13 does not stand alone but has a whole army at its disposal, 'God does not restrain his anger; even the cohorts of Rahab cowered at his feet.' In chapter 26:11–13 this is a monster God battles with and subdues, 'The pillars of the heavens quake, aghast at his rebuke. By his power he churned up the sea; by his wisdom he cut Rahab to pieces. By his breath the skies became fair; his hand pierced the gliding serpent.' The word translated 'gliding serpent' in v.13—'*nahash*'—is exactly the same word used to describe the serpent in the Garden of Eden. Here is a being which brings about death, had an army of helpers and can take the form of a wily serpent.

Rahab the sea monster is also to be found in Psalm 74:13–14, 'You divided the sea by your might; you broke the heads of the sea monsters on the waters. You crushed the heads of Leviathan; you gave him as food for the creatures of the wilderness.' This chaos monster is arrogant and proud, inhabiting the depths of the sea. In Scripture the sea is a symbol for all that is dark and unruly standing in opposition to God. This is the domain in which this creature exercises his rule.[6]

We are therefore forced to ask: who, according to Scripture, stands implacably opposed to God's rule, bringing death, chaos and destruction in his wake? Who is the enemy of God's people looking for someone to devour and destroy?

The features of the Leviathan in vv.18–21 also offer clues as to its true identity, 'His sneezings flash forth light, and his eyes are like the eyelids of the dawn. Out of his mouth go flaming torches; sparks of fire leap forth. Out of his nostrils comes forth smoke, as from a boiling pot and burning rushes. His breath kindles coals, and a flame comes forth from his mouth.' Where do you think the idea of a fire breathing dragon came from? Here. In fact, the Greek translation of the

Old Testament, the Septuagint, actually uses the word 'dragon' instead of 'Leviathan' at this point giving it supernatural connotations.

The overwhelming size of this creature is brought out in verse 31ff, 'He makes the deep boil like a pot; he makes the sea like a pot of ointment. Behind him he leaves a shining wake; one would think the deep to be white-haired. On earth there is not his like, a creature without fear.' This reaches the murky base of the world, the underworld if you will, and it is so huge that even the vast expanses of the oceans are churned into foam by the creature's thrashings. This is the creator of chaos, fear and misery. 'The description overwhelms the imagination, piling feature upon feature to create an impossible image, thereby conceiving the inconceivable monstrosity ... Its descriptive language combines different elements that are categorically exclusive of one another, and thereby jams the imagination's ability to form a complete picture of the monster.'[7]

The revelation in Revelation

It is in the New Testament that all these images finally come together giving us the full identity of this supernatural creature, Revelation 12:9 says, 'The great dragon was hurled down—that ancient serpent called the devil, or Satan, who leads the whole world astray.' Now we begin to see more clearly who is behind it all.

I am reminded of the Rolling Stones song, 'Sympathy for the Devil.'

Please allow me to introduce myself
I'm a man of wealth and taste
I've been around for a long, long year
Stole many a man's soul and faith

And I was round when Jesus Christ
Had his moment of doubt and pain
Made sure that Pilate
Washed his hands and sealed his fate

Pleased to meet you
Hope you guess my name
But what's puzzling you
Is the nature of my game

I stuck around St Petersburg
When I saw it was a time for a change
I killed the Czar and his ministers
Anastasia screamed in vain

I rode a tank
Held a general's rank
When the Blitzkrieg raged
And the bodies stank

Pleased to meet you
Hope you guess my name.

Have *you* guessed the name of the Leviathan?
It is Satan.

Pulling back the curtain on evil

Perhaps we can now begin to see what God is doing with Job as he embarks upon a graphic description of this wicked creature let loose in the world. Might he not in effect be saying to Job something along these lines: 'Yes, your instincts were right back in chapter 9:24 when looking around at the chaos in the world and in your own life you asked, "If it is not he (God), then *who* is it?" Whilst there is only one God and no second god, nonetheless there is another "who"—a supernatural being working his wicked way—his name is Satan. This is the monster who effectively appears again and again in your life Job—behind the bandits who attacked your farm, the death inflicted on your family, the disease crippling your body and yes, even, in the guise of your so called friends who kicked you when you were down with lies and half-truths, and even the one most closest to you, your wife when she urged you to curse me and die.' The enemy is being unmasked, not in a straightforward way, but by using powerful and evocative imagery which Job might be able to grasp at least in some measure.

If there is a personal malevolent spiritual being who is instrumentally responsible for so much of the wickedness in the world and to which men and women surrender themselves, albeit unwittingly, when they choose to sin, that begins to make some sort of sense. Of course it pushes the question one stage back: where did this creature come from in the first place? God could not have made a creature evil otherwise he would be the author of evil. But what if he had made a good creature which turns evil, such that evil is self-generating?

We saw that the creature's most striking features are described in 41:18–21 'His sneezings flash forth light, and his eyes are like the eyelids of the dawn. Out of his mouth go flaming torches; sparks of fire leap forth. Out of his nostrils comes forth smoke, as from a boiling pot and burning rushes. His breath kindles coals, and a flame comes forth from his mouth.' Is this not similar to what we have seen of God in chapters 9 and 38? There we see displayed the power and splendour of God revealed through what he has made—the lights in the heavens and the quaking of the earth in what is called a *theophany*. Here we have a creature mimicking that. This actually takes us to the heart of the nature of evil and the nature of sin and how such a creature like Satan came into being in the first place.

Evil as 'unmaking'

God did not 'make' evil, because evil does not have the kind of substantial existence that good has. Good can exist all by itself, but evil can't. Evil is parasitic on the good in that if there were no good, there would be no evil, but it is possible to have good without evil. For example, one could imagine a perfectly good orange and beside it an orange which has gone bad, infected by a fungi. While it is possible to have the good orange without the bad, one cannot have the bad without it being formerly good. Or we may think of blindness as the absence of sight and just as blindness is the departure from sight, so sin is the departure from good. Here, then, evil is more of an 'unmaking' of what is good, a corruption. Accordingly, evil desires parody good desires. Gluttons desire food which is a perversion of the eating instinct. Despots might want good things for their country such as harmony and prosperity. But what makes them evil is that wrong motives drive them and wrong means are employed to procure them. When things don't occupy their rightful place in God's scheme of things that is when they *become* evil.

Therefore, if evil is a good thing misappropriated, an 'unmaking' of the good, then we might have some idea of how evil may have come about in the first place. Suppose a good personal being chooses to try and occupy a position he shouldn't in God's universe? Choosing is a good thing, but what is chosen—a position to which one is not suited—makes it a bad thing. When that happens this choosing has a corrupting influence on the whole character of the chooser, so that the creature itself becomes bad. You can't ask the question what made the creature choose the bad in the first place, because by definition a choice is just a choice. To be 'made' to choose something is a contradiction in terms. The person decided to act irreducibly. Sure, all sorts of factors are taken into account when deciding what to do, but at the end of the day all you can say is that a person chose. This understanding of the nature and origin of evil was developed by Augustine of Hippo and popularised by C.S. Lewis in his *Mere Christianity*.

Let's turn to one more part of Scripture to help clarify our understanding, Isaiah 14:12–15, 'How you are fallen from heaven, O Day Star, son of Dawn! How you are cut down to the ground, you who laid the nations low! You said in your heart, "I will ascend to heaven; above the stars of God I will set my throne on high; I will sit on the mount of assembly in the far reaches of the north; I will ascend above the heights of the clouds; I will make myself like the Most High." But you are brought down to Sheol, to the far reaches of the pit.'

The Babylonians had a myth in which the 'bright shiner' *Heylel*, the name given to the planet Venus, tried to become King by scaling the mountain ramparts of the heavenly city, only to be vanquished by the all-conquering sun. That picture is taken, reapplied and given a new twist by Isaiah, for it now applies to the King of Babylon and his arrogance to be the all-conquering King. This king is inordinately proud, having aspirations to world domination. In short he wants to be God. In Job 41:34 we read of the Leviathan, 'He looks down on all that are haughty; he is king over all that are *proud*' (NIV). Could it not be that behind this picture in Isaiah of a human being we have a shadowy picture of an earlier angelic being who also aspires to be like god? The Hebrew word, *Heylel*—'bright shiner' or 'Venus'—is translated in the Latin version of the Bible, the Vulgate, as 'Lucifer.' You can't help but notice the arrogance in the words 'I will ... I will ... I will ...' Satan works most effectively by mimicking God. God promotes his will by words—giving commands and making promises—so does Satan. God overawes people with spectacular signs and miracles—so does Satan. But they are all inferior to God; they don't quite match up to him (v.20).

Satan has his limits too

One of the main points of chapter 41 is not simply that there is a malevolent spiritual being at work in the world and behind the scenes, but that this being does not lie *outside God's rule*. This is underscored in the first eleven verses and the claim in v.11 that 'Everything under heaven is mine.'

In his book, *The Serpent of Paradise,* Erwin Lutzer writes: 'The devil is just as much God's servant in his rebellion as he was in the days of his sweet obedience ... We can't quote Luther too often: The devil is God's devil. Satan has different roles to play, depending on God's counsel and purpose. He is pressed into service to do God's will in the world; he must do the bidding of the Almighty. We must bear in mind that he does have frightful powers, but knowing that those can only be exercised under God's direction and pleasure gives us hope. Satan is simply not free to wreak havoc on people at will.'[8]

As we saw in chapter 1, Satan was given permission to test Job, but limits were set by God. Of course Satan would like us to believe that he has unlimited power for his power depends on us believing the lie. But when we see that he is like a snarling dog we have to pass by on our way to heaven, but who is chained, then we begin to see things quite differently.

For one thing you don't get too close to a snarling dog even if it is on a chain. Yet Christians fail to see this, foolishly they think they are somehow immune from the temptations of others and only discover they are not when it is too late. The devil knows our weaknesses far better than we do, but at least if we recognise some of them we should be careful to avoid situations which might aggravate them. To play around with Satan is as foolhardy as playing around with a rabid Rottweiler! The lesson is obvious—keep your distance.

The other thing is to keep close to him who has defeated Satan and who holds the chain—the Lord Jesus Christ. It is as we dwell on his love, promises, power, and victory found at the cross where Satan has been trussed up like a turkey for Christmas that our real strength is found. Of course it was to be Job's experience that it was only as he encountered God face to face and heard his voice that a quiet peace and turnabout of events took place. As the old hymn puts it: 'Turn your eyes upon Jesus.'

The strength the believer should derive from knowing God's mastery over evil and its defeat at the cross has been wonderfully expressed by Christopher Ash, '[The] assurance that he [God] can do all things and that no purpose of his can be thwarted is the comfort I need in suffering and the encouragement I crave when terrified by evil. He does not merely permit evil but commands it, controls it, and uses it for his good purposes. ... [The] God who knows how to use supernatural evil to serve his purposes of ultimate good can and will use the darkest invasion of my life for his definite and invincible plans for my good in Christ.'[9]

A refining instrument

In the early church John Chrysostom placed the issue of suffering within the wider context of God's providential purposes, which includes God's use of Satan as an instrument in order to refine his people. He writes, 'For as a gold refiner having cast a piece of gold into the furnace allows it to be proved by the fire until such a time as he sees it has become purer: even so God permits the souls of men to be tested by troubles until they become pure and transparent and have reaped much profit from this process of sifting; wherefore this is the greatest species of benefit.' With regard to the work of Satan, this is seen as a means used by God to develop and mature the character of believers and so magnify the ministry of the gospel in the world: 'Nevertheless, though the devil had set so many traps, not only did he not shake the church, but instead made her more brilliant. For during the period when she was not troubled she did not teach the world as effectively as she now does to be patient, to practise self-restraint, to bear trials, to demonstrate steadfast endurance, to scorn the things of the present life, to pay no regards to riches, to laugh at honour, to pay no heed to death, to think lightly of life, to abandon homeland, households, friends, and close relations, to be prepared for all kinds of wounds, to throw oneself against the swords, to consider all the illustrious things of the present life—I am speaking of honour, glories, power and luxury—as more fragile than the flowers of springtime.'[10]

More to come

However, the presentation of God's mastery over evil forces in these chapters goes beyond his instrumental use of the devil to bring about his good purposes for his people in the world. There is more than an indication that such forces will be defeated and there even being joy in its anticipation; 'YHWH is allowing that there is a great evil at loose in his creation, but he promises one day to defeat it (40:19, 41:8). In fact, YHWH "raises the stakes" in this chapter by giving Job a close-up picture of an evil which Job is aware of (Job refers to Leviathan in 3:8) but cannot fully comprehend. It is as if YHWH directs Job's gaze to a massive, writhing monster which Job cannot even touch, much less engage with in combat. Only Behemoth's maker can bring a sword near to kill it (40:19) and only YHWH can and will engage in battle with Leviathan (41:8) … There is a kind of staggering joy driving the description of Leviathan. Perhaps that is the monster's ultimate defeat, that our Saviour is not only unintimidated by his opponent, but positively cheerful as he looks forward to the day when he pierces the fleeing serpent (26:13). What would it be to view creation with that kind of irrepressible, divine joy, before the redemption of all things?'[11]

Viewing 'creation with that kind of irrepressible, divine joy' was seen in the life of Bishop Stanway.

This godly Bishop had been used by God to multiply churches in East Africa. In Tanzania alone he was responsible for establishing twenty dioceses and in retirement helped found a theological college in North America. D.A. Carson writes of him in these terms: 'But when I met him, he had returned to his native Australia and Parkinson's disease had so debilitated him that he could no longer talk. He communicated by writing on a pad of paper, more precisely he could no longer write, but printed his answers in scarcely legible block letters. By the time I got to know him a little, I felt emboldened to ask him how he was coping with his crippling disease. He had been so active and productive throughout his life; how was he handling being shunted aside? He had to print out his answer on that pad of paper three times before I could read it: "There is no future in frustration."' Carson adds, 'Bishop Stanway would not allow himself the luxury of frustration. He lived with eternity's perspective before him and frustration plays no part there. He simply had not tied his ego to his service, so that when the active, fruitful forms of service he had enjoyed for decades were withdrawn, he himself was not threatened. He could still trust in his Master and pursue what was best within the constraints imposed on him.'[12]

God's good purposes for his people—like Job—can't

be frustrated by evil, by whatever form it is expressed. In anticipating the final defeat of the 'Leviathan' already in evidence in his own earthly ministry which he shared with his disciples and which led them to experience something of the 'irrepressible divine joy,' Jesus remarks, 'I saw Satan fall like lightning from heaven. Behold, I have given you authority to tread on serpents and scorpions, and over all the power of the enemy, and nothing shall hurt you. Nevertheless, do not rejoice in this, that the spirits are subject to you, but rejoice that your names are written in heaven' (Luke 10:18–20). This is the one thing the 'Leviathan' can never take away and in which believers can rest secure.

7 Faith Fulfilled

Job 42

JOB HAS BEEN ON A ROLLER COASTER OF A JOURNEY, ONE which has more or less taken him to the gates of hell and back—at least that is what it felt like.

Job's attitude began with a mixture of self-pity and self-assertion. As his life was devastated by one calamity after another, not surprisingly Job sank into himself in grief. Then, in spite of his wife's advice to curse God and die, he insisted on defending his own innocence. By way of contrast the attitude recommended by Job's three friends was self-accusation. 'Come on, Job,' they said, 'admit that you are suffering because of your sin. This is God's judgement upon you, repent and your fortunes will soon be returned.' But Job refused to be bullied into signing such a false confession which was tantamount to surrendering his integrity—he was an innocent sufferer. The fourth counsellor then entered the fray, Elihu, who urges upon Job another attitude to adopt, that of self-discipline. He tries to get Job to see that there may be some purpose in his pain which is not to be construed as retribution but instruction, God's way of disciplining and correcting. Finally, it is God who speaks and the only attitude which is left open to Job is self-surrender, falling before God in reverence and humility: 'Therefore I despise myself and repent in dust and ashes' (42:6).

Faith seeking understanding

When Job speaks of 'despising' himself, it could mean 'reject' or 'loath' (cf. 9:21), that is, he is ashamed of the way he has been thinking about God and portraying him by the way he has spoken. And by speaking of 'repenting,' the idea is of wishing he could take his words back, for example when he had said of God, 'I do not believe he would give me a hearing. He would crush me with a storm and multiply my wounds for no reason' (9:16–17 NIV).[1] He also refers to 'dust and ashes,' a reference to the fact that he is but a creature and so *can't* know everything unlike the great Creator. As we have seen, one of the problems of our own making is that when confronted with things we don't understand we try to put together some half-baked explanation with inadequate information. The result is often a distorted view of God, for example, 'God the cosmic child abuser' as some have blasphemously suggested. Job realises that he has sailed quite close to the wind in what he has said and now regrets it.

This underscores one of the main lessons of the book: know your own limitations, 'Faith seeks understanding, and faith builds on understanding, but faith does not finally depend upon understanding. This is not to say, of course, that faith is intrinsically irrational (quite the contrary), but that faith takes us into realms where explanations fail us—for the present.'[2]

No other ending

For some it seems almost incredible that after such a robust wrestling with the problem of suffering in which the most forthright candour has been expressed in challenging traditionally cherished beliefs, the writer seems to throw it all away by rounding off the story with what amounts to a fairy tale ending of the 'they all lived happily ever after' variety (some think the ending was tagged on later by an editor). Fairy stories may have happy endings, but real life often does not. To tell us that Job ends up with more than he had originally is a cop out at best and a contradiction at worst, suggesting the retributive theory is correct after all: be naughty and you get punished, be good and you get rewarded (if you hang in long enough).[3]

I want to suggest that no other ending would have been possible if the theological integrity of the book is to be maintained. For if we had simply finished with God's encounter with Job, God's wisdom and power may have been vindicated, but not his justice which, after all, was Job's primary concern.

In this epilogue we see both the justice of God and the grace of God meeting each other in action.

Prayer answered

To begin with we see God's justice in the way he deals with Job's three friends, as we see in 42:7–9:

> After the LORD had spoken these words to Job, the LORD said to Eliphaz the Temanite: "My anger burns against you and against your two friends, for you have not spoken of me what is right, as my servant Job has. Now therefore take seven bulls and seven rams and go to my servant Job and offer up a burnt offering for yourselves. And my servant Job shall pray for you, for I will accept his prayer not to deal with you according to your folly. For you have not spoken of me what is right, as my servant Job has." So Eliphaz the Temanite and Bildad the Shuhite and Zophar the Naamathite went and did what the LORD had told them, and the LORD accepted Job's prayer.

Job was vilified over and over again and his character impugned by these well-meaning but misguided friends. He was accused of being a hypocrite, of harbouring wicked thoughts and gaining his wealth through sharp practice. That had been so painful for Job it had torn him apart. But the more Job protested, the more convinced his so called friends became that he was hiding something: 'he protests too much' it seemed. He desperately needed someone to come to his defence;

someone who knew the truth and would testify to his innocence. But there was only one who could do that, and that was God—which was the heartfelt cry of chapter 9.

That is precisely what we see God doing here— answering Job's prayer. He rounds on Job's three counsellors because of what they have said. They may have been sincere in their beliefs, but sincerity is no defence when truth is at stake. They were wrong in what they had claimed about Job and, more to the point by implication, they were wrong in what they had said about God. It is ironic that they thought they were defending God, while all the time they were misrepresenting him. Their theology reduced God to an inconsistent despot. Such a view of God is simply not right. It is those of us who are zealous for the truth who need to be very careful that we do not find ourselves holding out to others a false view of God for the sake of a tidy theology which permits no loose ends, perhaps by focusing on his justice to the exclusion of his grace or, as is more likely today, focusing on his love to the exclusion of his justice. Such an appalling false image will not go unnoticed by God. Rather, we are to go with the entirety of God's self-revelation and not our neat, tidy and, often, inadequate thoughts about him.

Ultimate vindication

Job is being vindicated in time, but that is not always the way it works out for believers. We may well be misunderstood and misrepresented, even by some of our Christian friends, and will have to live with the pain. But there will come a day when everything will be out in the open, when there will be a clearing of the books—and that will be judgement day. Then the record will be put straight. The lies and half truths, those sneers that we may have had to endure, not only because we have owned the name of Jesus Christ but because we had the courage to put our faith into practice when other Christians faded away, will be acknowledged. In the meantime it is not for us to be preoccupied with trying to clear our name and justify ourselves. Instead we are to get on with what God has called us to do and leave the judging up to him who alone is well placed to do it.

Triumphant grace

However, not only do we see God's justice at work but also his grace. If God had treated Job's friends according to strict justice, as they had been arguing God *must* treat everyone according to the retribution principle, they would have been snuffed out in an instant! But that didn't happen. To be sure, sin had to be covered over, and that involves a sacrifice (v.8). What is more, someone is needed to intercede for sinners, someone of good standing whom God will hear. The only one who filled all the requirements was the one they had been slandering as a liar and a cheat—Job. What irony!

To Job's credit, he did pray for them and God accepted

his prayer. For Job there was no malice or resentment as far as we can tell and no exacting revenge. Instead, there was kindness. I wonder how many of us would have been gracious enough to behave in that way. Often, when someone says a bad word against us we don't forget it, and we make sure they don't forget it either. Not Job—he prays for them.

Surpassed restoration

What is more, we see God's grace shown to Job by the way his former life is not simply restored but surpassed: 'And the LORD restored the fortunes of Job, when he had prayed for his friends. And the LORD gave Job twice as much as he had before' (42:10).

It is important that we understand this correctly and don't see it simply as a form of 'compensation' for all that Job has suffered. At the beginning of the saga it was Satan's complaint to God that the only reason why Job was religious was because of what he could get out of it, that there was some base ulterior motive at work, he was 'in it for what he could get out of it.' But by taking everything away from Job, God demonstrated that the accusation had no real foundation. Even when Job had nothing to entice him to believe in God, he still trusted him, admittedly with some struggle. It wasn't a matter of Job thinking, 'If only I can just hang on in there for a while there might be some goodies in store.' Job didn't know what the outcome was going to be; in fact it was more than likely that he thought he was going to die in this state. Nevertheless he still trusted God and so became an example to follow according to the Lord's half-brother James in his letter, 'As you know, we count as blessed those who have persevered. You have heard of Job's perseverance and have seen what the Lord finally brought about. The Lord is full of compassion and mercy' (James 5:11).

Refined and restored

What was it that the Lord finally brought about? Two things: a refined character and a restored life.

First, a refined character

It was the Satan's taunting of God that the reason why Job was so good was because his circumstances were too good. That may or may not have been the case because the only way to know whether it was so or not was if those things were taken away. But with them having been removed in such a traumatic way, travelling through what some call 'the dark night of the soul,' by the end Job emerges as a wise man *par excellence* who is devoted to God because God is God and is worthy as such, seeing him as the one who, while at times is silent, is still present and at work in and through all he has made—even the Leviathan! The God Job has come to know at the end of his suffering is much greater and more sublime than the one he believed in before his trial began. But it was only by journeying through the suffering that such a transformation took place. Susannah Ticciati argues that, 'we have to understand Job's obedience as exploration. As we expressed it aphoristically above: Job's self is in the process of its probing. But this means that his obedience, sanctification, or integrity is best understood, not primarily about being or becoming anything, nor primarily about doing anything, but about being transformed. Job's integrity is constituted by his ongoing transformation.'[4]

Isn't this often our experience? When is it that prayer becomes deeper, the Bible more meaningful and Christian fellowship most precious? Is it when everything is hunky dory? No, it is when we are being tried, that is when we experience God in quite a different way and at the end value him all the more.

Second, a restored life[5]

Is not what we have at the end of Job what we see at the end of the Bible in the Book of Revelation, a restoration and surpassing of all that is good in the aftermath of great evil and suffering? As Carson rightly observes, 'The blessings that Job experiences at the end are not cast as rewards that he has earned for his faithfulness under suffering. The epilogue simply describes the blessings as the Lord's free gift. The Lord is not nasty or capricious. He may for various reasons withdraw his favour, but his love endures for ever … In that sense, the epilogue is the Old Testament equivalent to the New Testament's anticipation of a new heaven and a new earth. God is just and will be seen to be just.'[6]

We have to remember that the book of Job appeared early on in the history of Israel, before any clear ideas about the afterlife had been revealed, although there is an inkling of the possibility of a future life as we see in 19:25–27: 'For I know that my Redeemer lives, and at the last he will stand upon the earth. And after my skin has been thus destroyed, yet in my flesh I shall see God, whom I shall see for myself, and my eyes shall behold, and not another.' Therefore, just as it was only by God vindicating Job in time rather than at the end of time that justice was seen to be done, so it is only by God blessing Job in this world that it can be shown that the righteous life is worth it after all for it is the truly blessed life.

A reflection of the reality

What we see with Job is a pale reflection of what will be our experience in heaven as believers.

Job had his heart's desire fulfilled, he met with God. That encounter changed everything; he saw everything, his blessings and his trials, in a new light because he saw God. Then the life he started to live was a far richer, fuller one than the one he lived before (42:12). At the beginning of the story it was Job who used to go far away to feast with his children, but now his children, family and friends come to him for feasting and consolation, bringing him gifts and gold for all that he suffered (42:10–11). Isn't that something like heaven? There is the presence and meeting of God who is the source of all joy and delight and there is the meeting of the Christian family whose being reflects the love and joy of God as he radiates his glory through them. This is how the American theologian Jonathan Edwards describes the full satisfaction which Job experienced in part but which we shall experience in full: 'How blessed are they that do see God, that are come to this exhaustless fountain! They have obtained that delight that gives full satisfaction; having come to this pleasure, they neither do nor can desire more. They can sit down forever and ever, and desire no change. After they have had the pleasures of beholding the face of God millions of ages, it won't grow a dull story; the relish of this delight will be as exquisite as ever.'[7]

Job's pleasure was eventually to come to an end (42:16); but that is when his real pleasure was about to begin when he met his God again, but this time not in a tempestuous storm, but a celestial city.

If Job could put his trust in God amidst such torment, how much more so those who believe in the God who has been through torment in the person of Jesus Christ? 'So also saints in the new covenant, when they find themselves in deep pain that seems to have no point, will find themselves saying with Job, 'Though he slay me, yet I will trust him' (13:15). Like Job, we endure (James 5:11), 'not in serenity and tranquillity, but in the energy to persist in faith … in the midst of contrary experiences.' And like Job, they too will be vindicated for it (42:7–10). This is God's expectation for us when we suffer in a Job-like way: not to give up on God, and to wait for him to restore us, whether in this life or the life of the world to come.'[8]

8 *From Job to Jesus*

THERE ARE SO MANY MOVING MOMENTS IN THE BOOK
of Job. One of the most poignant is found in chapter
9. Job protests his innocence, desperate to put his case
before his Maker and yet he realises the futility of such
a desire, for God is not mortal who can be confronted
face to face as in a human court. What is more, even
if such an encounter were to be made possible, Job is
only too aware that he needs some kind of mediator
to allow such a meeting to take place: 'For he is not a
man, as I am, that I might answer him, that we should
come to trial together. There is no arbiter between us,
who might lay his hand on us both. Let him take his
rod away from me, and let not dread of him terrify me.
Then I would speak without fear of him, for I am not
so in myself' (9:32–35). The ideal mediator of course,
would be one who would not only represent Job fully,
capable of empathy, having 'walked in his shoes,' but one
who would be able to bring God 'up close and personal'
which would not lead to a mere mortal's destruction

in the face of white hot holiness. The New Testament's claim is that such a mediator exists and his name is Jesus: 'there is one mediator between God and men, the man Christ Jesus, who gave himself as a ransom for all' (1 Timothy 2:5).

It is the truth of the incarnation of the Son of God which enables us to 'know why we can trust the God who knows why' and answer the questions, 'How are we to think and speak of God when we suffer?' We are to think of God as the one who has suffered and so who is not 'unable to sympathize with our weaknesses, but one who in every respect has been tempted as we are, yet without sin' (Hebrews 4:15). As Ortlund rightly concludes, 'the ways in which the book of Job portrays and interprets suffering in God's economy anticipate and pre-figure the Lord Jesus.'[1]

In this final chapter we explore something of that anticipation and pre-figuring of Christ, seeing how we can move from Job to Jesus.

A type of one to come

The centrality of the second person of the Trinity becoming a man for men and so answering the desire of Job has been forcefully put by Dorothy L. Sayers: 'He [Jesus of Nazareth] was not a kind of demon pretending to be human; he was in every respect a genuine living man. He was not merely a man so good as to be "like God"—he was God. Now, this is not just a pious commonplace: it is not a commonplace at all.

For what it means is this, among other things: that for whatever reason God chose to make man as he is— limited and suffering and subject to sorrows and death —he [God] had the honesty and courage to take his own medicine. Whatever game he is playing with his creation, he has kept his own rules and played fair. He can exact nothing from man that he has not exacted from himself. He has himself gone through the whole of human experience, from the trivial irritations of family life and the cramping restrictions of hard work and lack of money to the worst horrors of pain and humiliation, defeat, despair, and death. When he was a man, he played the man. He was born in poverty and died in disgrace and thought it well worthwhile.'

She continues, 'So that is the outline of the official story—the tale of the time when God was the underdog and got beaten, when he submitted to the conditions he had laid down and became a man like the men he had made, and the men he had made broke him and killed him. This is the dogma we find so dull—this terrifying drama of which God is the victim and hero.'[2]

We have been following the trials of one who is both 'victim and hero'; subject to 'the worst horrors of pain and humiliation,' the man Job. In Jesus, the God who became man without ceasing to be God, all of these things are recapitulated and surpassed. Jesus is the righteous sufferer par excellance—God's servant tested to the limit, whose suffering was cast by onlookers within the framework of the retribution theory and

who defeated the Behemoth (death) and the Leviathan
(Satan) decisively at the cross and who eventually will
restore all things to a state of shalom only tasted by Job
in his restoration.[3] But rather than going directly from
Job to Jesus in the Gospels we shall take a more indirect
route via the Suffering Servant of Isaiah 52–53 where
we are given three different perspectives of the Lord's
Servant pre-figured by Job.

A 'friends' perspective

First, there is the Lord's servant as *men* see him, namely
as a figure of pitiful contempt. At the beginning of
his descent into the emotional abyss, isolated on the
ash heap, Job was barely recognisable to his friends in
his anguish; when they saw him from a distance, 'they
could hardly recognise him'. Isaiah saw a similar figure,
'As many were astonished at you—his appearance was
so marred, beyond human semblance, and his form
beyond that of the children of mankind' (Isaiah 52:14).
So physically grotesque is this man in his agony that
people can't even bare to look at him, they turn away
their faces in shear disgust as one might turn away from
the corpse of a rotting dog lying by the road side, 'as
one from whom men hide their faces he was despised,
and we esteemed him not' (Isaiah 53:3b). His face is
so battered that he is hardly recognisable as a human
being at all, he looks more like a monster than a man.
Even when this Servant first started out in life there
was nothing particularly special about him, 'he had no
form or majesty that we should look at him, and no

beauty that we should desire him' (Isaiah 53:2b). Had you met him in the street you would have simply passed him by as being of no consequence. But not now, not as he hangs there on full public display, impaled on the gallows.

And so as with Job's friends the question arises: 'Why the suffering of this man?' Just as Job's comforters reached for the retribution theory to explain Job's torment, so do those who look upon this other Servant of the Lord in Isaiah 53:4b 'yet we esteemed him stricken, smitten by God, and afflicted.' 'God would never treat a good man like this,' they reason, 'he must have been especially morally vile for God to inflict such a punishment.'

But as with Job, the irony is that what they were witnessing was the suffering of an innocent man, 'he had done no violence, and there was no deceit in his mouth' In other words, his sufferings are completely undeserved. Consequently not only is he a figure of contempt in the eyes of the world, he is also a figure of tragedy in 53:7, 'He was oppressed, and he was afflicted, yet he opened not his mouth; like a lamb that is led to the slaughter, and like a sheep that before its shearers is silent, so he opened not his mouth.' Here is a gentle man who had never lifted a finger to hurt anyone being led like sheep to the abattoir with no chance of escape, only to be abused and discarded. He is the vulnerable prey of an unjust world which feeds on those poor gentle souls who will not stick up for themselves. Unlike

Job he is a young man, according to Isaiah 53:8, still in the prime of his life with no children to bear his name into posterity (and, of course after the desolation of the storm, neither had Job). But more than all of these, here is an innocent man guilty of no crime of his own, 'he had done no violence, and there was no deceit in his mouth' (Isaiah 53:9). Cast out and left to die on the local rubbish tip inhabited by vermin just as Job found himself cast out scratching at his sores on the local dung heap. As far as the world is concerned it is a senseless and pathetic waste of a life. This is how men see him, as men saw Job, a tragic figure, somehow deserving his fate encompassed by the laws of divine retribution—good men are rewarded and wicked men punished.

God's assessment

We then move on to another anticipation of the Servant-King as displayed in the life of Job, the innocent suffering God's wrath to fulfil God's purposes. This is the Servant as *God* sees him in Isaiah 52:13f, 'my servant shall act wisely; he shall be high and lifted up, and shall be exalted … Kings shall shut their mouths because of him.' Where the world sees ignominy and humiliation, God sees wisdom and achievement. God, as it were, has to scan the whole spiritually barren world to find one man, pushing his way up through the unprofitable, hard earth of human depravity, like a small shoot (Isaiah 53:2), forcing its way up through the hard sun-baked earth to do the work no one else could do. Remember how the Satan had been roaming to and fro throughout the earth and it is to Job, God's servant, that he is directed as an example of a truly righteous man (1:7–8)? Here we have God's answer to the question, 'Why?' Why is this man suffering in Isaiah 53:10, 'Yet it was the will of the LORD to crush him; he has put him to grief; when his soul makes an offering for guilt, he shall see his offspring; he shall prolong his days.' The idea of God inflicting pain on the innocent is set out as something redemptive—pain with a purpose.

One of the deep cries of Job was for justice to be done and seen to be done. That is what the prophet perceives as happening in the events surrounding the Servant of the Lord. He speaks of a 'guilt offering.' For centuries the Jews had been carefully schooled by God that before sin could be forgiven a sacrifice had to be offered. The blood spread on the surface of the altar symbolised in the most vivid terms the appalling penalty that sin demands death. In almost every case when the Bible uses the word 'blood' what is signified is not the life of the animal but its death and often a violent death at that.[4] It is offered to expiate sin (covering it) and propitiate God (turning away his anger). This was something Job knew of hence the offering of sacrifices for his children and later for his friends (1:5; 42:8). However, what we see here is something which goes way beyond anything any God-fearing Jew would dare to contemplate. This is not an animal butchered on an altar but a man hanging on a scaffold. That which was expressly forbidden by the Law of Moses is now being carried out by God himself, namely, a *human* sacrifice offered for sin.

A believer's view

This leads to the third perspective, the Servant as *believers* see him. This corresponds to the readers of the Book of Job. The reader knows of Job's innocence as declared by God. The reader is also aware of the heavenly court and the 'wager.' The discredited retribution theory is also in mind. The onlooker knows that God is not acting capriciously but purposefully, deepening Job's knowledge of himself and so transforming Job. Similarly at the heart of this piece of poetry, the Servant Song, we see that God's purpose in the suffering of his Servant is to bring about true knowledge of God and a lasting transformation—not of the Servant, but those who would believe on the Servant and receive his kindness as the three counsellors received the kindness of Job. Isaiah 53:4–6 says: 'Surely he has borne our griefs and carried our sorrows; yet we esteemed him stricken, smitten by God, and afflicted. But he was pierced for our transgressions; he was crushed for our iniquities; upon him was the chastisement that brought us peace, and with his wounds we are healed. All we like sheep have gone astray; we have turned—every one—to his own way; and the LORD has laid on him the iniquity of us all.' That 'we' who are healed is the same 'we' that considered him stricken by God in v.4. The prophet anticipates that at least some will come to understand the divine purpose of his death. 'Who has believed what he has heard from us?' asks the prophet in 53:1 and 'to whom has the arm of the LORD been revealed?' the answer is that some will. 'Oh yes,' they will say, 'we too at one time had nothing but contempt for this Jesus, as Job's friends had contempt, but not now.' Because of the gift of faith they see the divine logic of it all. It was not this man who was guilty but us. It was not Job who had failed to speak the truth about God, but his friends such that they needed a mediator, the intercession of a righteous man. Similarly when someone realises they have not spoken the truth about God, perhaps denying his justice or downplaying his grace; in Jesus, the true mediator, forgiveness can be found and a deep transformation experienced.

As well as transformation, there is also restoration in Isaiah 53:10b–12: 'he shall see his offspring; he shall prolong his days; the will of the LORD shall prosper in his hand. Out of the anguish of his soul he shall see and be satisfied; by his knowledge shall the righteous one, my servant, make many to be accounted righteous, and he shall bear their iniquities. Therefore I will divide him a portion with the many, and he shall divide the spoil with the strong, because he poured out his soul to death and was numbered with the transgressors; yet he bore the sin of many, and makes intercession for the transgressors.'

Room for rewards

Job's restoration following his suffering was, as we have
seen, an act of grace, not compensation. On the other
hand, whilst a believer can and, perhaps should, pursue
what is good without ulterior motives of self-gain
(religion as cloaked self-interest),[5] we should be careful
not to push this point too far since there is a strand of
biblical teaching which points to rewarding faithfulness
as a means of encouraging perseverance.[6]

The pursuing of righteousness for its own sake as
a Christian virtue is captured by the hymn of
Francis Xavier:

My God, I love thee, not because
I hope for heaven thereby;
Nor yet because who love thee not are lost eternally.

Nor with the hope of gaining aught,
Not seeking a reward ...
Solely because thou art my God
And most loving King.

Job has shown that in many ways this is what he has
been doing, contrary to the Satan's claim. Of course
it is only in the crucible of suffering that we often
discover what God really does mean to us, when all else
is stripped away. But it doesn't follow that while love of
God (who himself is the reward) is to be uppermost in
the life of a believer, other inducements to faithfulness
can't play their part.

One place where this clearly is the case is in the Letter to the Hebrews. The writer is seeking to encourage a group of believers to persevere in the faith amidst hardship, something they had known before (10:32–34) and refers to obtaining a reward as an incentive for remaining faithful in the recent round of persecution, 'Therefore do not throw away your confidence, which has a great *reward*' (10:35). Encouragement to suffer is couched in terms of rewards. Indeed, Jesus himself is put forward as a model to follow in this regard, together with saints of old:

> Therefore, since we are surrounded by so great a cloud of witnesses, let us also lay aside every weight, and sin which clings so closely, and let us run with endurance the race that is set before us, looking to Jesus, the founder and perfecter of our faith, who for the joy that was set before him endured the cross, despising the shame, and is seated at the right hand of the throne of God. Consider him who endured from sinners such hostility against himself, so that you may not grow weary or fainthearted. (Hebrews 12:1–3)

The section we have been looking at in Isaiah may be part of the background for this teaching in Hebrews. The Servant will see his offspring (earlier in chapter 2 of Hebrews the presentation of 'many sons to God' is seen as some of the fruit of Jesus' death); could not this be part of the joy set before Jesus?

Whilst rewards are not to be a kind of bait to dangle

before people to become believers in an evangelistic event, they surely do play their part when enduring suffering as believers, to know there is a good end in view. The Apostle Paul similarly appeals to future glory in order to encourage Christians on in the faith, 'So we do not lose heart. Though our outer self is wasting away, our inner self is being renewed day by day. For this light momentary affliction is preparing for us an eternal weight of glory beyond all comparison, as we look not to the things that are seen but to the things that are unseen. For the things that are seen are transient, but the things that are unseen are eternal' (2 Corinthians 4:16–18).

Job's 'rewards' of a restored family were 'external' to his suffering as it were, whereas the rewards of the Servant are internally related to his suffering in the sense that they are a consequence of them—the justification of many who are the offspring of his sacrificial death having taken away their sin.

We saw in the last chapter that the restoration and indeed, the surpassing of Job's fortunes, are anticipatory of the new heaven and earth as presented in the New Testament where, 'Behold, the dwelling place of God is with man. He will dwell with them, and they will be his people, and God himself will be with them as their God. He will wipe away every tear from their eyes, and death shall be no more, neither shall there be mourning, nor crying, nor pain anymore, for the former things have passed away' (Revelation 21:3–4). The Behemoth of death will have been defeated by the Suffering Servant King, as anticipated in Job 40, swallowed up in his victory, 'The sting of death is sin, and the power of sin is the law. But thanks be to God, who gives us the victory through our Lord Jesus Christ' (1 Corinthians 15:56–57), thus fulfilling Isaiah 53:11–12. What is more, the Leviathan, the devil, who holds all men in fear of death (Hebrews 2:14–15) will also be no more, 'and the devil who had deceived them was thrown into the lake of fire and sulphur where the beast and the false prophet were, and they will be tormented day and night forever and ever' (Revelation 20:10).

Our suffering brother

Job has been described as 'the world's classic sufferer and the one in whom all sufferers know that they have at least one brother who understands their pain.'[7] In the light of the coming of Christ, prefigured by Job, we can go further and say in him we have a *God* who understands our pain. If Job had sufficient warrants to trust the God of all wisdom and so think and speak of God properly, how much more so do we because of the full revelation of God in his Son and the glory of the cross?

The reasonableness of trust lies in the known trustworthiness of its object. And on-one is more trustworthy than the God of the cross. The cross assures us that there is no miscarriage of justice or of defeat of love either now or the last day. 'He who did not spare his own Son, but gave him up for us all—how will he not also, along with him, graciously give us all things?' (Romans 8:32). It is the self-giving of God in the gift of his Son which convinces us that he will withhold nothing from us that we need, and allow nothing to separate us from his love (vv.35–39). So between the cross, where God's love and justice began to be clearly revealed, and the day of judgement when they will be completely revealed it is reasonable to trust in him.[8]

Therefore with even greater confidence than Job we can say that because of Jesus: 'I know that my Redeemer lives, and at the last he will stand upon the earth. And after my skin has been thus destroyed, yet in my flesh I shall see God, whom I shall see for myself, and my eyes shall behold, and not another (Job 19:25–27).

Notes

Preface

1. Cited by Os Guinness in *Long Journey Home: A Guide to Your Search for the Meaning of Life* (Doubleday, 2001), p. 65

2. Viktor Frankl, *Man's Search for Ultimate Meaning* (Perseus, 2000), p. 19

3. Cited in Craig G. Bartholomew and Ryan P. O'Dowd, *Old Testament Wisdom Literature: A Theological Introduction* (Inter Varsity Press, Apollos, 2013), p. 165

4. Eric Ortlund, 'Five Truths for Sufferers from the Book of Job,' *Themelios*, Vol. 40, Issue 2 (2015), p. 253

Chapter 1

1. Elie Wiesel, *Night* (Penguin, 1981)

2. A.R. Eckardt, 'The Recantation of the Covenant' in A.H. Rosenfeld and I. Greenberg, eds, *Confronting the Holocaust: The Impact of Elie Wiesel* (Bloomington: Indiana University Press), p. 163

3. There are basically two views of what constitutes 'free will.' There is the libertarian position which allows for 'absolute power to the contrary'; we must be free to choose between opposites. One proponent of the libertarian view is philosopher William Hasker who defines it as 'An

agent is free with respect to a given action at a given time if at that time it is within the agent's power to perform the action and also in the agent's power to refrain from the action.' The alternative position is 'voluntarism' or the Augustinian/Edwardsian view which is defined by Sam Storms as 'The ability to act according to his inclination and desires without being compelled to do otherwise by something or someone external to himself.' In other words we simply choose according to our nature.

4. Harold S Kushner, *When Bad Things Happen to Good People* (Anchor; Reprint edition, 2004)

5. Philip Yancey, *Where is God When it Hurts?* (Zondervan, 1977)

6. M. Volf, 'Taking God to Court,' *Christian Century*, Vol. 115, Issue 35 (1998), p. 1222

7. Craig G. Bartholomew and Ryan P. O' Dowd, *Old Testament Wisdom Literature: A Theological Introduction* (IVP Apollos, 2013), p. 318

8. Os Guinness, *Doubt* (Lion, 1976), p. 199

9. Craig G. Bartholomew and Ryan P. O' Dowd, *Old Testament Wisdom Literature: A Theological Introduction*, pp. 130–31. The original language also reflects the content in another way according to Herman Wouk, 'the craggy, sometimes tortured Hebrew eerily calls up the agony of a just man on the rack of an unjust experiment performed by Satan with the incomprehensible permission of God.' in Os Guinness, *Unspeakable* (Harper, 2005), p. 203

10. Gerald Wilson in his *Job*, NIPC (Hendrickson, 2007), pp. 41–42 suggests that Job may have been plagued by fear all along.

11. 'I refer to "the Accuser" above because it better captures the nuance of טשה לַ for an ancient Israelite audience than "Satan." The noun with the definite article refers to a role, not a proper name. Within the context of the entire canon of Scripture, I do identify this figure

with Satan in the NT (cf. Revelation 12:9); but since ancient Israelites would not have been able to draw these connections, I prefer the more general term "the Accuser" when discussing the book of Job.' Eric Ortlund, 'Five Truths for Sufferers from the Book of Job', *Themelios*, Vol. 40, Issue 2, (2015), p.254

12. See John H. Walton, 'Job,' *The NIV Application Commentary* (Zondervan, 2013) p. 64, '*hassatan*'—Challenger.

13. John H. Walton, 'Job,' *The NIV Application Commentary*, p. 39

14. Bartholomew and O'Dowd, *Old Testament Wisdom Literature*', p. 134

15. D.A. Carson, Going Beyond Clichés: Christian Reflections on Suffering and Evil,' https://www.youtube.com/watch?v=A1OfE6fFLvI accessed 3 December 2018.

Chapter 2

1. Quoted by John Stott, *The Cross of Christ* (Inter Varsity Press, 1986), p. 312

2. Robert Alter in his *The Art of Biblical Poetry* (New York: Basic, 1985), p. 90 concludes, 'Job's cosmic poetry, unlike that of his Friends, has a certain energy of vision, as though it proceeded from some immediate perception of the great things it reports.'

3. 'We miss the point of the triple cycle of debates between Job and his friends unless we recognise that he shares with them the major premise that God rewards the good and punishes the wicked: their minor premise is that Job has suffered greatly, from which they conclude he has sinned greatly; his minor premise is that he is innocent, and his conclusion that something has gone badly astray in the divine dispensation of justice. The resolution comes when the voice of God from the whirlwind sets before Job a panorama of mystery in

the natural world, which cannot be fitted into his tidy anthropocentric world-view, and so enables him to break out of his religious orthodoxy into a new vision of God beside which his old religion appears second-hand … The hypothesis must be altered to fit the facts, not the facts wrested to fit the hypothesis.' G.B. Caird, *The Language and Imagery of the Bible* (Oxford: Duckworth, 1980), pp. 15–16

4.   Steven Nation, 'Is God good? A Study on the Person and Work of Yahweh in the Book of Job,' *Churchman*, Vol. 123, Issue 4 (2009)

5.   Kathryn Schifferdecker, *Out of the Whirlwind: Creation Theology in the Book of Job* (Cambridge, MA: Harvard Theological Studies, 2008), p 107

6.   Edouard Dhorme, *A Commentary on the Book of Job* (Thomas Nelson, 1984 [original 1926]), p. cxxxv

Chapter 3

1.   Lewis made a distinction between a 'supposal' and an allegory. A supposal is an invitation to try seeing things in another way, and imagine how things would work out if this were true. Here is how Lewis describes the difference: 'If Aslan represented the immaterial Deity in the same way on which Giant Despair represents despair, he would be an allegorical figure. In reality however, he is an invention giving an imaginary answer to the question, "What might Christ become like if there really were a world like Narnia and he chose to become incarnate and die and rise again in that world as he actually has done in ours?" This is not allegory at all.' In Alister McGrath's *C.S. Lewis—A Life: Eccentric Genius, Reluctant Prophet* (Hodder and Stoughton, 2013), p 278

2.   R. Fyall, *Now My Eyes Have Seen You: Images of Creation and Evil in the Book of Job*, New Studies in Biblical Theology Vol. 12 (IVP, 2002)

3. John H. Walton, 'Job,' *The NIV Application Bible* (Zondervan, 2012), p.187

4. 'The evidence, then, identifies Leviathan with Satan, the culmination of various guises in which he has appeared, for example: Leviathan (3:8); Yam and Tannin (7:12); Sea (9:8 and 38:8–11); Rahab (9:13 and 26:12); the gliding serpent (26:13), R. Fyall, *Now My Eyes Have Seen You*, p. 168

5. Os Guinness, *Unspeakable: Facing Up to Evil in an Age of Genocide and Terror* (Harper Collins, 2005), p.217

6. For a detailed and helpful exposition of this chapter, see Fyall, *Now my Eyes have seen you*, pp 44–54. He writes, 'This passage, with its formidable theological freight and its clear links with the heavenly court scene of the prologue and with 'seeing God' in the epilogue, has a visionary even revelatory character. To put it another way: Job's glimpse here of the realities of the divine council that set the plot in motion and his vindication by God at the end show that this is supremely a passage in which he has spoken what is right.' p. 50

7. This is a legal term (*mokiah*) that refers to someone who argues a case and negotiates on behalf of another. John H. Walton, 'Job,' *The NIV Application Bible*, p. 172

Chapter 4

1. Robert Alter, *The Art of Biblical Poetry* (New York: Basic, 1985), p. 91

2. R. Fyall, *Now My Eyes Have Seen You* (IVP, 2002), p. 53

3. D.A. Carson, *How Long O Lord?* (IVP, 1990), p. 170

4. Alter, *The Art of Biblical Poetry*, p. 92

5. This is not to deny that Elihu has not bought into the retributive theory shared by Job and his friends, see 36:11, 'if they obey and serve him [God] they will spend the rest of their days in prosperity and

their years in contentment. But if they do not listen they will perish by the sword and die without knowledge.'

6.   D.A. Carson, *How Long O Lord?*, p. 169

7.   C.S. Lewis, *Mere Christianity* (Fount, 1978), p. 171

8.   Cited by Peter Lewis, *The Lord's Prayer: The Greatest Prayer in the World* (Paternoster, 2008), p. 192

9.   John Hick, 'An Irenean Theodicy' *Encountering Evil*, Ed. S.T. Davies (T and T Clark, 1981), pp. 38–52

10. Gregory A. Boyd, *God of the Possible: A Biblical Introduction to the Open View of God* (Baker Publishing, 2000) and John Sanders, *The God Who Risks: A Theology of Providence* (Inter Varsity Press, 1998).

11. Archibald MacLeish, *J.B: A Play in Verse* (Houghton Mifflin, 1958), p. 126

12. Carson, *How Long O Lord?*, p. 171

13. Jerry Sittser, *A Grace Disguised* (Zondervan, 1996), p. 199

14. David C.K. Watson, *In Search of God* (Inter Varsity Press, 1974), pp.54–55

15. John Piper, https://www.desiringgod.org/interviews/how-should-i-read-the-book-of-job accessed 3 December 2018.

16. Eric Ortlund, 'Five Truths for Sufferers from the Book of Job,' *Themelios*, Vol. 40, Issue 2 (2015), p.257. Ortland goes on to unpack the pastoral implications of this third category of suffering, 'Attention to this aspect of the book of Job deepens and nuances how we interpret suffering and prevents us from well-intentioned torture of our friends who suffer, either by implicitly blaming them for their pain or by reducing their tragedy to moral lessons. The word "torture" may seem extreme, but that is how Job experienced the "help" of his "friends" (19:22). After all, anyone who has (for instance) suffered the loss of a child and then been blamed for it, or been told God is trying to

teach them something, knows how bitter that kind of "help" is (cf. 6:5–7). When walking with a friend through traumatic suffering, it may be appropriate to find a time to ask if there is some sin which God is bringing to the surface, or some growth edge which this pain is exposing. But if one's friend cannot find any unconfessed sin or area in which spiritual growth is needed, the friend may be undergoing a Job-like experience' (p. 257).

Chapter 5

1. C.S. Lewis, *God in the Dock: Essays on Theology* (Fount, Collins, 1979), p.100

2. P.C. Craigie, 'Biblical Wisdom in the Modern World; III. Job,' *Crux*, 16 (1980), p. 8

3. Cited in Os Guinness, *Unspeakable* (Harper San Francisco, 2005), p. 197

4. See John Walton and Andrew Hill, *Old Testament Today* (Zondervan, 2004), p. 307

5. G K Chesterton, 'The Book of Job' in *Selected Essays* (Wilco, India, 2009), p. 93

6. Michael V. Fox, 'Job 38 and God's Rhetoric,' *Semeia* 19 (1981): pp. 53–61

7. D.A. Carson, *How Long O Lord?* p. 172

8. Eric Ortlund, 'Five Truths for Sufferers from the Book of Job,' *Themelios*, Vol. 40, Issue 2 (2015), p. 259. Similarly, Steven Nation writes, 'God's responses to Job's speeches in chapters 3–37 commences with a defence of His person and work by pointing to creation and showing how He is not an anarchist or a God of disorder but a God of stability and precision. His first speech (38:1–40:2) compares Job's insignificant power and God's omnipotence. Yahweh declares that the world is not as disorderly as Job supposed. His second speech

(40:7–41:34) highlights God as the great Creator and sustainer who has the strength to overcome chaos and maintain order.' 'Is God good? A Study on the Person and Work of Yahweh in Job,' *Churchman*, Vol. 123, Issue 3 (2009), p. 322

9. Eleonore Stump, 'Faith and the Problem of Evil,' in *Seeking Understanding: The Stob lectures 1986–1998* (Grand Rapids: Eerdmans, 2001), pp. 524–25

10. Os Guinness, *Unspeakable* (Harper San Francisco, 2005), p. 205

11. Daniel J. Estes, 'Communicating the Book of Job in the Twenty-First Century,' *Themelios*, Vol. 40, Issue 2 (2015), p.248

12. The so called 'scientific method' of Ernst Troeltsch (applying the criteria of criticism, analogy and correlation to a purported account in the Bible) automatically ruled out the miraculous, for criticism assumed the account is false until proven true; analogy that something contemporary must be found which is analogous to the event described, and correlation, the event must be the result of earlier events. By definition, the miraculous does not conform to such criteria. This doesn't mean that the miraculous is impossible, but that the criteria are faulty.

13. Alvin Plantinga, *Warranted Christian Belief* (New York, Oxford University Press, 2000), pp. 497–98

14. 'Through his encounter with God, Job is addressed in the deepest part of his being, in what the Old Testament wisdom calls the heart. Such heart knowledge exceeds logical understanding but is no less real and, at least, according to Job, more fundamental and more important.' Craig G. Bartholomew and Ryan P. O' Dowd, *Old Testament Wisdom Literature: A Theological Introduction* (IVP Apollos, 2013), p. 156

15. John Piper, https://www.desiringgod.org/messages/job-reversal-in-suffering accessed 3 December 2018

16.   Ibid., p 148

17.   Eric Ortlund, 'Five Truths for Sufferers from the Book of Job,' *Themelios*, Vol. 40, Issue 2 (2015), pp. 257–8

Chapter 6

1.   D.J.A. Clines, *Job, A Bible Commentary for Today*, Ed. G.C.D. Howley (London: Pickering & Inglis, 1979), pp.559–92

2.   See Fyall, *Now My Eyes Have Seen You* (IVP, 2002), pp. 127–74, who uses ANE Canaanite lithology to argue that Behemoth and Leviathan sustain the presence of death, evil and the Satan figure in Job 1–2. As Ortland wryly comments, 'Failure to recognize the supernatural symbolism of these animals short-circuits the rhetorical strategy of these chapters. If YHWH is describing his prowess only over two animals which one might visit in a zoo, the speech becomes irrelevant to Job, not to mention a little pathetic. What is a man mourning dead children supposed to say to a deity who boasts of capturing a hippo.' Eric Ortlund, 'Five Truths for Sufferers from the Book of Job', *Themelios*, Vol. 40, Issue 2, (2015), p.260

3.   R. Fyall, *How Does God Treat His Friends?* (CFP, 1995), p. 119

4.   Some would use the literary category of 'myth' to describe the imagery being used. There is no fundamental objection to this so long as we understand what we mean by the term 'myth.' Fyall writes, 'By 'myth' I do not mean a story which is 'make believe,' rather an attempt to embody in narrative the great truth of good and evil, of origin and consummation. Of truth and error.' in R. fyall, *Now My Eyes Have Seen You*, p. 27. G.B. Caird, likens myth to a lens whereby the user says to his audience, 'Here is a lens which has helped me understand the world in which we live and how God relates to it; look through

it yourself and see what I have seen.' He writes that it is 'referential in the same fashion as a metaphor is referential. It tells a story about the past, but only in order to say something about the present and the future.' *Language, Imagery and the Bible* (Duckworth, Oxford, 1980), p. 224. John J. Bimson, like Fyall, argues 'that Behemoth and Leviathan are mythical chaos monsters representing cosmic forces hostile to God and inimical to human welfare.' John J. Bimson, 'Fierce Beasts and Free Processes: A Proposed Reading of God's Speeches in Job' in *Wisdom, Science and the Scriptures: Essays in Honour of Ernest Lucas*, Ed, Stephen Finamore and John Weaver (Pickwick Publications, Oregon, 2014), p. 18

5. J.C.L. Gibson, *Job* (St Andrew's Press, 1985), p. 254

6. In Isaiah 27:1 the same symbol is used to depict evil rulers who threaten God's people with captivity, as did Pharaoh of old. God promises to deliver his people from such a monstrous tyrant: 'In that day, the LORD will punish with his sword, his fierce, great and powerful sword, Leviathan the gliding serpent, Leviathan the coiling serpent; he will slay the monster of the sea.'

7. T.K. Beal, *Religion and Its Monsters* (Routledge, 2002), p. 52

8. Erwin Lutzer, *The Serpent of Paradise: The Incredible Story of How Satan's Rebellion Serves God's Purposes* (Moody, 1998)

9. Christopher Ash, *Job: The Wisdom of the Cross, Preaching the Word* (Wheaton, IL: Crossway, 2014), p. 424

10. Cited in Christopher A. Hall, *Learning Theology with the Church Fathers*, (Inter Varsity Press, 2002), pp. 183–205

11. Eric Ortlund, 'Five Truths for Sufferers from the Book of Job', *Themelios*, Vol. 40, Issue 2 (2015), p.260

12. D.A. Carson, *A Call to Spiritual Reformation*, (Inter Varsity Press, 1992), pp. 140–141

7

H. Walton, 'Job', *The NIV Application Bible* (Zondervan, 2), p. 432

Christopher J.H. Wright, *The God I Don't Understand: Reflections on Tough Questions of Faith* (Grand Rapids: Zondervan, 2009), p. 22

'For many, the ending seems too contrived, as though Job lived happily ever after, even though observation would suggest that life after tragedy is not always or even often like that. In fact, severe traumas typically leave lifelong wounds and scars. Even more troubling, the book raises profound ethical questions: How could a loving and just God allow Job to be treated so badly? What about Job's children and servants and animals—don't they count for something? Are humans just pawns in a cynical cosmic debate between God and the adversary?', Daniel J. Estes, 'Communicating the Book of Job in the Twenty-First Century', *Themelios*, Vol. 40, Issue 2, (2015), p.246

4.   Susannah Ticciati, *Job and the Disruption of Identity: Reading Beyond Barth* (T&T Clark, 2005), p. 170

5.   'Job is restored and blessed materially and relationally more than he was at the beginning. The narrative arc is one of implacement to displacement to much deeper implacement. Job and Ecclesiastes, serve not only to deal with the exceptions to the character-consequence motif of wisdom but also to indicate that the journey into depth implacement that wisdom calls forth may involve immense suffering.' Bartholomew and O'Dowd, *Old Testament Wisdom Literature* (IVP Apollos, 2013), p. 324

6.   D.A. Carson, *How Long O Lord?*, pp. 176–77

7.   In *Jonathan Edwards: Heaven and Hell*, Ed, Strachen and Sweeney, (Moody Publications, 2010), p. 95

8. Eric Ortlund, 'Five Truths for Sufferers from the Book of J↳ *Themelios*, Vol. 40, Issue 2 (2015), p 258

Chapter 8

1. Eric Ortlund, 'Five Truths for Sufferers from the Book of Job,' *Themelios*, Vol. 40, Issue 2, (2015), p.262

2. Dorothy L. Sayers, *Creed or Chaos? and Other Essays* (Methuen, 1954), pp.1–2

3. The approach taken here is a literal-typological one, whereby the authorial intention of the original writer is taken seriously (hence the literal) and that all Scripture speaks of Christ by way of events and persons (hence typological). See Kevin J Vanhoozer, 'Augustinian Inerrancy: Literal Meaning, Literal Truth, and Literal Interpretation in the Economy of Biblical Discourse,' in *Five Views of Biblical Inerrancy*, Ed. J Merrick (Zondervan, 2013), p.232

4. 'From these figures it is clear that the commonest use of dām is to denote death by violence, and, in particular, that this use is found about twice as often as that to denote the blood of sacrifice. ... As far as it goes, the statistical evidence indicates that the association most likely to be conjured up when the Hebrews heard the word 'blood' was that of violent death.' Leon Morris, *The Apostolic Preaching of the Cross* (Inter Varsity Press, 1965), pp. 113–4

5. In ethics this is known as the 'deontological view' (derived from the Greek for 'necessary'—what ought to be), here the stress is on duty regardless of outcome. You just do 'the right thing.'

6. In ethics this would fall within the 'consequentialist view'—certain actions will result in certain outcomes.

7. Os Guinness, *Unspeakable* (Harper San Francisco, 2005), p. 203

8. John Stott, *The Cross of Christ* (Inter Varsity Press, 1986), pp. 328–9